$THAT$ $POSITI$

A practical philosophy for the promotion
of spiritual evolution.

By Harry Sylvester

Drawings by Annette Kelly

Printed on 100% recycled paper

1

THAT POSITIVE SPIRIT

© 1997 Harry Sylvester

Published by:
    Golden Eagle Publishing
    PO Box 4048
    SUDBURY
    Suffolk
    CO10 0HY
    England.

ISBN 1 902043 00 6

First Edition Published 1997

Printed and bound by the National Society for Epilepsy,
Chalfont St Peter, Gerrards Cross, Bucks, England. SL9 ORJ.

THIS BOOK IS DEDICATED

TO ALL THOSE WHO ARE SEARCHING

FOR LIGHT AND HARMONY

IN A CONFUSED WORLD

A list of organisations, publications, and groups, who at the time of going to press, were felt to be sympathetic towards the aspirations expressed in this book, are listed on the closing pages.

FROM THE AUTHOR

I have been asked to explain very briefly in basic English, just what this book was all about. Here goes!

At heart, everybody in the world would like to get on with everybody else, but the possibility for doing so is hindered by a pre-occupation with self.

If ambitions for human fraternity were given a priority from 'play school age', the world's children would instil harmony into human relations as never before!

To achieve such world camaraderie, much traditional thinking will need to be jettisoned, and replaced with a new positive philosophy which brings holistic considerations into all our thinking and decision making.

At present, we are in a stage of transition with old treasured values and attitudes being replaced by others. Naturally, there is concern about our ability to move into the Coming Age in a spiritually enlightening manner.

My book offers a philosophy which shows how the process of 'soul enhancement' can be universally accepted with enthusiasm and adopted so our arrival into the Coming Age will be smooth and overflowing with peace, compassion and harmony.

Acknowledgements

My thanks go to my family for their support and patience for the 'unsocial hours' involved in the lengthy compilation of the book. Special thanks go to my daughter, Annette Kelly, for her superb illustrations, which, in my view, bring words to life. But the constant encouragement from my friend, John Crowe PhD, cannot easily be expressed in words. Thank you John!

Harold Sylvester. 1997.

C O N T E N T S

FOREWORD

INTRODUCTION

PART ONE

Basic aims of the Positive Spirit Philosophy
Beginners guide to Positive Spirit
What is Positive Spirit?
Positive Spirit-the need for it
Positive Spirit-prospects for growth
Sceptics galore
Not a fantasy!
Changing history
Squeezing the evil out!
The Childhood Effects
Peace Child
Positive Spirit heals
Positive Thinking Plus
Think and Reflect

PART TWO

Positive bedtime thinking
The 'Diana effect'
Not so 'different' people
Be happy, don't worry, be friendly!
Harmless excitement
Being a parent
Courtesy is catching

Taming our aggression
Calling all celebrities
Keep your cool
Interfaith trend
Greetings challenge
Breaking the crime cycle
'I could be you!'
You can change the world!
Laughing tonic
One 'Godhead'
Infants of today, shapers of tomorrow
Daily soul challenge
Energy to spare?
Plug into goodwill and radiate
Unemployment, no stigma
Enjoy your food?
How to love yourself
Time Clock for Peace
Optimism wins through!
Bullying at school
Under-achiever?
Meditate and contemplate
"There is a fly in my soup!"
Compassion is strong
One race, the human race
Shy do-gooders
All the same 'underneath'
Hate out, love in
Childline is your line
Value Good Nature
Employers please note
Been made redundant?
Positive awakening thoughts

PART THREE

Bridging the God gap
Does God hear us?
Unifying those different
God, the universal power source
Once upon a time
Meditation, a PS springboard
Prayers for peace
Oneness in the eyes of Bahai

PART FOUR

Souls in action
Positive thoughts
Self-esteem in our hands
Bomb maker with a soul
Taming our aggression
Holistic awareness for bosses
Laughter on the NHS
Shoe exchanging
That unselfish trend
What's this love all about?
Our senses today and tomorrow
Spirituality Age on its way!

PART FIVE

Birthing spiritual values
What now education?

8

FOREWARD

Some positive thoughts came along. By the author:-

I was approaching three score years and ten, when I felt a strange urge to do something useful for mankind with my last few years. Like most people, I had been exploiting life to the full and, so far, had 'given back' very little. But what could an ordinary mortal do that would make an iota of difference to an ailing world?

In retrospect, this impulse have started sixty years ago, during which time my first introduction to lateral thinking came as a boy, when I met someone who confided in me his belief in an afterlife. I kept this from my Mother, but it was a momentary glimpse into the unusual, and must have sowed a seed for lateral thinking.

My second introduction to alternative ideas, was during my student days at Wye Agricultural College, when I met up with an organic farmer, who convinced me that we should be working with nature, rather than intent on mastering it. Another lateral thinker!

This led to my interest in the Soil Association, the embryo of the organic movement, which I joined in 1950. This was formed by Lady Eve Balfour, a biologist and practical farmer. It's aim was to enhance and study the vital relationships between the soil, plants, animals and humankind.

I did not realise it then, but the Soil Association was the fountainhead of today's holistic trends within ecology. It most certainly sowed the seed in my spiritual thinking process, but it took 35 years or so for me to realise the connection and implications.

My support for this organisation was still considered somewhat eccentric at that time, because organic husbandry was considered to be old fashioned.

Furthermore, subsidies and profit encouraged the 'quantity' concept of farming at the expense of 'quality', which fertilisers, pesticides and herbicides encouraged.

The Soil Association foretold the impoverishment of the countryside and it's wildlife, but, in the farming community, there was a luke warm response to the idea of abandoning sprays and artificial fertilisers, which gave such high crop returns. Not so with gardeners on the allotments, as they reacted warmly to demonstrations of composting, many turning to organic principles of cultivation. The healthiest food for the family was their priority.

In the 1960's, my ideas and those of my colleagues, were still seen to be a little offbeat, but environmentalists were now supporting organic agriculture as part of the up-and-coming green movement, which we had been supporting from it's infancy.

There was telling evidence from such groups as Greenpeace and Friends of the Earth, that we were poisoning the land, sea, and air with the toxic by-products of industry and intensive farming practices.

By the 1980's, ecology was front-page news in the world's media, and organic cultivation was perceived as being the ultimate need. Planting trees and returning the hedgerows to encourage wild life was officially given a green light. For the first time the environment was now a world issue. There was now a realisation that destroying trees in Brazil was just as harmful to the environment as unfiltered factory smoke from Derby.

Organisations such as Earth Action now began to relate the exploitation of the earth's resources with exploited tribes in remote regions, injustices under repressive regimes, and the need to ban modern weapons.

I would dearly like to know how many thousands of other people had been drawn into various forms of spirituality from green considerations, because I now believe they are inseparable.

These developments had taken a spiritual turn in the author's life, albeit not consciously until the late 1980's when I felt that peace and harmony of the human spirit was to be my main concern during my last years. I aimed to set up a movement to bring this to fruition.

At first, the enormity of the task, seemed so daunting as to appear ridiculous. Was I not suggesting that average mortals, like myself, could perform wonders when so many with more 'expertise' had failed?

Yet, questions burned in my mind. Maybe, we have all been looking in the wrong places for our salvation!

What is the purpose of our life on earth?

Do we arrive on this earth merely to be born, raise a family, and pass on, full stop?

At my agricultural college at Wye, we were taught that a good farmer should always try to leave his fields more fertile than when he found them. Likewise, could it not be that each one us has a duty to try and put 'something good' into the world and leave it a better place before we leave it?

From somewhere, I must have been heard, because a stream of sensible and practical ideas emerged in my mind, of which, strange to say, I do not claim to be the originator.

Since the 'messages of wisdom' had arrived 'on my doorstep' in my late years, I assume that I have been given the brief to start a trend and join others with similar aspirations and goals who will carry it to a conclusion.

Sceptics may dismiss the spiritual aspects of my revelations as wishful thinking, but although visionary by inclination, I claim to be rational, and not taken to bouts of fantasy.

Furthermore, I have complete conviction that the philosophy of Positive Spirit, has 'come to me' to do something about it, but please note, I am only a messenger, and not the creator.

It is my belief that you, the reader of this sentence, may well be able to receive 'positive messages of guidance' providing you open your minds to the possibility.

In years to come, I am convinced that thoughts travelling on high-frequency wave bands, will have some scientific acceptance, and such phenomena will be observed as being natural, and in no sense paranormal.

All those who aspire to religious faith, believe in communication at some level with their God, so messages over the 'spiritual network' from unofficial sources, should have some credence.

But it does seem strange that in spite of the many talented and intelligent people in the world, real peace and tranquillity has eluded us.

The explanation could be that we have numerous specialists, all expert in their own subject and so bound up with them that they are unable to bring the whole scene into focus. Matters of the spirit are left to the experts in the religious fraternity and physical activities are left to politicians and scientists.

What then is the message which comes over 'my radio'?

It is rather complicated, but in simplistic terms, we all want to be loved and to give love, not just the sexual kind but the caring style of love which comes from the soul. We hide these feelings at a subconscious level, but they come to life when the soul is stimulated by emotional events when we suddenly become unselfish, thoughtful and caring.

The aim of the Positive Spirit Philosophy is to self activate souls into 'permanent active service'. This will encourage people in all walks of life to make decisions with holistic considerations built into them. In due course, such aspirations within decision making, will become quite natural and part of the evolutionary process.

We have the power bestowed on us to bring this evolutionary step that much closer. There is no time like now!

Note.

During the compilation of this book, which has taken several years to complete, it was gratifying to find that other people hold similar aspirations to those expressed in this book. Readers may be encouraged to know that this information is being co-ordinated and networked so as to be most effective in spreading peace and harmony on a universal scale.

INTRODUCTION

TODAY, PEOPLE ARE BEWILDERED by the range of spiritual beliefs and are inclined to feel more secure in believing what they are taught to believe rather than question the meaning of their own spirituality.

I will satisfy your curiosity by telling you what the philosophy of Positive Spirit is not.

It emphatically is not another cult, religion, sect or con, and is non-profit making.

Having cleared such misconceptions, let me start with what most of us agree upon, namely that there is a spark of goodness in every living person. But taking this one stage further, there is a growing number of people who believe that spiritual power can be self-generated and promote a new vibrant harmony in human relations.

My aim is to introduce to the average man, woman and child, new and exciting ways for bringing all people in the world into a communal loving fellowship. Naturally, there are obstacles to be overcome.

In a world where confrontation is the norm, the idea of being able to create a universal 'goodness', will at first appear to be most unrealistic. It did to me at first.

Even optimists have been dismayed to find that modern man is still cruel, greedy, violent and often devoid of compassion. All this, in spite of some wonderful advice handed down over centuries by sages, prophets and range of religious instruction.

By now, spiritual wisdom should have created that elusive harmony we so desperately seek.

What has happened, is that in this modern age, only material things have become meaningful, and spiritual ones are viewed more as crutches to keep us on a Godly path.

Right across the globe, only cosmetic appreciation is given to Godliness, in spite of the fact that all scriptures proclaim the need to 'only do to others what you would have done to you'. Ministers of world religions must admit that, so very often, their followers only pay lip service to such sentiments.

Yet, there is a spark of Godliness always within us but held captive under the pressures of human activities.

Soul growth can only really take off universally when it becomes inspirational, creative, and enjoyable, so in effect it becomes a spiritual achievement of one's own making, rather than accepted as an antidote 'for our wickedness!'.

But most of us are not conscious of any 'soul power', so we don't know how to recognise it, let alone expand it.

So, I seek to expose this unrecognised potential for soul growth which lies within every human, irrespective of their faith, origin, colour, status, or geography.

The starting point for soul growth lies in the minds of children. You see, the philosophy of PS needs to be sown in the souls of the young so it can expand into the adult world.

At present, ethics, love, compassion, goodwill, justice, and humility are fed to our children in a most haphazard manner and this positive material is in competition with adult egoistic tendencies

The aim is to 'raise soul activity' at an early age so holistic tendencies become built into human behaviour more effectively. Thus, future generations will instinctively become more caring, and respectful of each other.

Let me be clear on one thing, the philosophy behind Positive Spirit does not seek to replace religions, but to link them together in a brotherly spiritual union. It is sad and so very unnecessary to see people with very similar caring beliefs, locked in strife and bloodshed over their different interpretations of Godliness. As I will show, original manuscripts of the diverse religions in the world have astonishingly similar spiritual goals.

Positive Spirit is catching and has the capacity to reach out to all corners of the earth like a spiritual chain letter. Those who practice it, feel an inner contentment which is indescribable.

Many people will at first question, "How can I, with my puny contribution, make an iota of difference to world strife?". To them, I say, "Nonsense, your soul, along with a billion others, can transform life on earth". This is no fantasy!

If you didn't know you had a 'little spark of God' inside you, get to grips with the idea right now. Yes, ordinary mortals like you and I, have soul power, which is needed in a world crying out for spiritual uplift.

If we all do nothing, we are part of the problem.
If we all do something, we are part of the solution!

Note:

All nett profit from sales of this book will be donated to organisations whose aim is to bring humans across the world into spiritual harmony and peace, irrespective of race, religion, colour, status, class, or ethnic origin.

Readers will find that some aspirations upon which the PS philosophy is based, have been repeated in a number of chapters. This is purposeful, as by request, such chapters are in demand for independent publication.

A personal note:

Some readers may feel that this book is rather patronising at times by its messages of 'how to live' and 'how to put the world right'. This may be due to the word YOU being used too often rather than the word WE or US.

Few people like to be told by someone else what is right or wrong for them and indeed some even object to 'professional advisors' moralising and appearing to talk down to them.

The PS revelations came to me late in my life and if they had come at an earlier time, I would have benefited and been a better and wiser person because of it.

Could it be that people who have experienced temptations and 'dipped their feet' in the negative world, are in a better position to judge what life is all about and able to talk about the problems along with the solutions?

Readers will need to search their own hearts and make up their own minds.

H.S.

PRINCIPLES OF THE POSITIVE SPIRIT PHILOSOPHY

BASIC AIMS OF THE POSITIVE SPIRIT PHILOSOPHY

PS will: -

Tell each person that they have latent 'soul power' which they can use for their own happiness and the well-being of those they meet, without being 'religious' in the conventional sense.

PS will:-

Foster compassion, love, and a caring concept in the minds of children, who will instinctively grow to become nicer people and pass on these traits to the next generation.

PS will :-

Extend the respect we are now giving to the animal kingdom, to include our own human species, and to create a loving fellowship between all peoples, irrespective of faith, race, status, or ethnic origin.

PS will : -

Act as a catalyst for peaceful solutions between countries and within countries where there is political and religious conflicts

PS will: -
Foster that 'little spark of God' which almost all people have within themselves, but don't realise it. From then on, self-worthiness will take on a new meaning of true happiness.

PS will:-
Bring religious faiths together by looking for the positive things they have in common, rather than the present trend for emphasising the differences.

PS will:-
Encourage the young to view the purpose of human life on Earth in a positive manner. Namely, that we should leave no stones unturned to find ways of leaving the world a little better place than when we entered it.

PS will:-
Sow a loving thought and reap the action from it,
Sow the action and reap a universal habit,
Sow the habit and reap a more loving world!

Part One

BEGINNER'S GUIDE TO POSITIVE SPIRIT

WHY THE NAME, POSITIVE SPIRIT? Let us look at this word, spirit, for it has several meanings. For instance:-

'He is a spirited fellow', means, 'he is full of life!"

'It lifts up one's spirit to see his quick recovery', means,

'It gives one joy to see him well again'.

'He has plenty of spirit', means, 'he has plenty of courage!'

'Holy Spirit' implies, 'an holistic precious life-force'

Spirit therefore contains a mix of valuable meanings.

But what of the word Positive? This implies being enthusiastic, forward looking, good and benign, so the combination of the two words, Positive Spirit, the abbreviation being PS, has a profound meaning, namely, the benign life force with unlimited potential for uplifting humanity.

PS is available to every human on the planet. There is no need to be clever or educated to possess it and one only needs to search one's heart to find it. Excitingly, it grows gently as it becomes used.

One way to set things in motion, is to first search one's heart, and check to see whether one's motivations are unselfish. One must sincerely want to see peace, love, and harmony in the world, in your home, or at your place of work, and most importantly, in one's own heart!

Bringing Positive Spirit into your life can be helped by knowing from whence it originates, and the criteria needed for expanding it.

It is the adoring attention from mother at birth, together with her conscious attention to one's welfare, which make souls receptive for PS to prosper.

Following on from this, providing one has received positive guidance, and fair discipline during adolescence, there is every likelihood that one will turn out to be a very caring person, with Positive Spirit ready for a further stage of growth in adulthood.

But not all children receive parental love and much adult behaviour negates favourable character trends.

The NSPCC and Childline report numerous cruelties to children on a daily basis, and without help before adolescence, bruised souls create a cycle of cruelty. Adults who are cruel to children almost always have been at the receiving end of the same in their childhood.

One of the aims of the PS philosophy is to break such negative cycles, and the healing element of PS is limitless. Even violent criminals have the ability to kick-start their souls into activity and be transformed into honest caring people.

Religious faith can help the process to a degree, but it is regretful that the isolation of modern religions do not show a unified path to spirituality in spite of the fact that their original scriptures portray a different picture of humanity. They quote, 'brothers and sisters of the human form should treat each other equally without favour, wherever their place of origin'.

In essence, we are all one human race and we must learn to accept with a sense of brotherhood, "different' people who inhabit our planet alongside us. Every human being has a soul base.

The philosophy of PS is concerned with making all people conscious and responsible for their own spirituality when most people are not even aware they have any, or even the right to think they have any!

Becoming aware of one's own spirituality does not come easily because we are are constantly reminded of our weak and sinful ways.

It is well known that low self esteem inhibits a person's potential. It may be academic achievements, scoring goals on the football field, or nowadays, just holding a job.

It is partly a question of raising people's faith in themselves, and releasing their soul power which has been held in suspension as it were.

It would not be out of place to stop praying for one's sins to be forgiven, but to pray for enlightenment as to how one's good points can be amplified. Say upon awakening, "I have the means of making the world a brighter place". Do not be too surprised to find that a role to help someone in need comes along and you feel great in your role as a 'mini-miracle worker'

It may sound simplistic, but soul power can be triggered into action by just being challenged. It never runs out of steam, because it is replenished and nourished by just putting it to work. It's as simple as that!

The source of this spirituality is from God's inexhaustible supply. A further way of explaining it, is by comparing your soul to a battery containing PS 'electricity'. Your soul is 'lit up' following a good deed, a loving thought or unselfish act. But 'the battery' never runs out, for it is always topped up by PS power. This means there is a constant supply of spiritual power always ready for you when you 'throw the switch'.

The media expresses so much negative material that you might doubt the very existence of this 'positive soul power' I refer to. How wrong you would be! Peace makers arrive on the scene of conflicts, whether it be in the Middle East, Ireland, South Africa, or Bosnia. Their success is often fragile, but some peace there is, where none stood before !

There are thousands of good motivated souls doing valuable jobs for charitable causes. True, few would admit to being driven that way by a conscious spiritual drive, but those who have performed a kind act or deed do admit to feeling good inside, a sort of feeling of contentment. (This must not be confused with some 'do gooders' who perform for praise or admiration)

This new concept of each of us being of value to the world in some shape or form, is exciting. It can be described as 'creative motivation of the soul.'

Some of you may well ask "How can humble me possibly perform any real service to mankind?" My reply is, "Make no mistake, most people have powers beyond their imagination, once they find the 'wave length' of caring, compassion and sincerity".

When a happy personality dominates the scene, a most miserable person can be caught up in the humour, and be transformed. In the same way, Positive Spirit can catch on in amazing ways, almost like a chain letter. It has an invisible aura which rubs off on others, without you or the recipients even faintly thinking about it.

But should you still doubt your spiritual self-worthiness, check it out on this questionnaire and test your PS rating:-

Your neighbour loses a child from a cot death.
Do you go out of your way to cheer her up?

'Positive' Sleep

Go to sleep
with the notion
that you can
make the world
a nicer place

Wake up and
be amazed to
find you want
to do that
very thing!

Part One

A cripple begs for money on the pavement.
Do you feel an urge to give something?

A blind person needs help to cross the road. Do you help him?

A starving child is shown on your TV screen.
Do you feel compassion and wanting to do something about it?

You kill a bird with your car. Do you feel upset?

If the answer is "yes", your Positive Spirit is active and ready for further development. Soul development is not hard work and it is enjoyable, because you are 'liking yourself' more and seeing the better nature of those whom you formerly disapproved In time, PS will have taken you over. You are just a nicer person all round.

WHAT IS POSITIVE SPIRIT?

THE PHILOSOPHY OF POSITIVE SPIRIT IS NOT a religion, cult, or a new dogma, and can be best be described by the effect it has on people. A series of questions portray the inspirations it generates.

What is it that brings redundant building workers to volunteer to rebuild an orphanage in Albania without pay?

What is it that brings people to man the telephone lines of the Samaritans?

What was it that brought tears to the eyes of hardened paratroopers, as they rescued Kurd women and children from the mountain sides in northern Iraq?

What inspired groups of people to help civilians caught up in the Bosnian war?

When people suffer a grievous loss, such as losing a dear one from an illness or accident, have you noticed how keen they are to support an organisation whose aim it is to prevent such a thing happening to someone else? Having 'felt' for their loved one, a distraught person now 'feels' for someone else who might meet a similar fate. That someone could be a total stranger and perhaps of a different faith, yet a kindly unselfish wish comes out of the void. That is Positive Spirit working!

Unselfish activities which come from the heart are spiritual in nature because they counter the egoistic nature of human beings who demand tangible advantage in almost everything they do.

The fact that people experience a profound fulfilment in helping others confirms the belief that PS will become a natural caring trait of a more caring human being. Taking this one stage further, it could well become a primary instinct of mankind.

Positive Spirit can be described as follows:-

IT IS A SPIRITUAL FORCE, WHICH HAS A PERMANENT SOURCE OF REPLENISHMENT. IT ACTIVATES COMPASSION, JUSTICE, LOVE AND A STRONG CARING ELEMENT. IT EXTENDS TO ALL HUMANS IRRESPECTIVE OF ETHNIC ORIGIN, RACE, RELIGION, SEX, COLOUR, STATUS AND GEOGRAPHY. IT ALSO CONVEYS THE UTMOST COMPASSION AND RESPECT FOR ANIMALS WITH WHOM WE SHARE OUR PLANET.

Part One

POSITIVE SPIRIT, THE NEED FOR IT

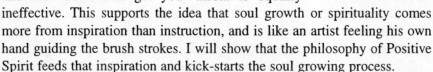

I HAVE SHOWN that Positive Spirit is already within us, albeit in a low state of activity.

The ultimate in PS has been exemplified by Jesus and Ghandi, but present trends towards a universal spirituality are frustrated by 'ego competition', the enemy of unselfishness.

History shows that we cannot be 'told to be good' and the 'devil will get you' threat is equally ineffective. This supports the idea that soul growth or spirituality comes more from inspiration than instruction, and is like an artist feeling his own hand guiding the brush strokes. I will show that the philosophy of Positive Spirit feeds that inspiration and kick-starts the soul growing process.

When souls are weak, they are squeezed into the subconscious by man's urge for excitement, achievement, and selfish power.

But mankind is not in the grip of an outside 'devil' as some would suppose. The supposed 'devil' is a victim of our incapacity to think positive and realise that our more saintly qualities, like the genie in the bottle, are just waiting to be released from it's restrained quarters.

Souls are ready to developed, but no-one has observed the mechanism to do it, one problem being that 'soul-power' is held down by feelings that no ordinary person is fit to claim spiritual status. Putting it another way, it is felt to be an 'impertinence to God' to feel 'holy' unless one has been blessed by a minister of religion.

People are hesitant in taking up charitable occupations in case they appear pious. They avoid ridicule by those who might comment, "Here's another do-gooder".

At the present time, one can see how humans around the world are in a state of limbo. For the most part, deep in their hearts, they know what is right or wrong, what is selfish or unselfish, what is kind or cruel, what is love or hate. They just need to get their act together at soul level, and act upon that knowledge.

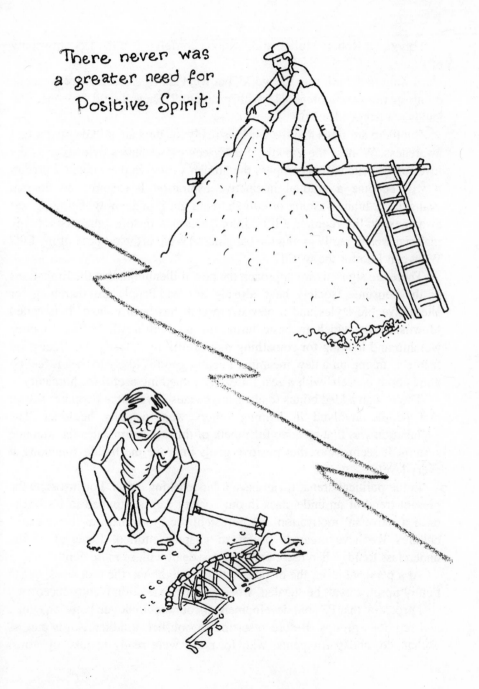

I quote Dr Robert Muller, addressing a conference at the UN University of Peace,

"I want to demilitarise the world, but what are these destructive weapons doing in the hands of people with problems? They should be squeezing hands not triggers!"

But there are signs that the world is ready to adopt an attitude of spiritual awareness. Witness the growth of the green movement which suggests the love for animals will encompass the human variety in due course. I predict it will become a gradual instinctive aspiration It requires no dogma, evangelism, brain washing or cult status to get it under way. Bringing self awareness to life requires a little introspection with some questions. Is my material wealth really giving me happiness? What is the purpose of my life? What can I do for the world?

There are signs, as we approach the new millennium, that the limitations of the consumer society have already arrived. People are searching for alternative life styles and a new expression has been coined. It is called 'downshifting' which in basic terms, means shifting down from money worship and looking for something more fulfilling. Clearly, the 'feel good factor' is taking on a new meaning. Feeling good is likely to mean 'feeling good about oneself' with a zest for doing something useful for humanity.

There is an added bonus to altruism, because a research team has shown that people involved in helping others were actually healthier. The explanation was that positive fulfilment of this kind stimulates the immune system. It seems, too, that positive goals improve the bodily functions at every level.

In the political arena, it can have a far-reaching effect. For instance, the present trend of an underclass in our society can be stopped in it's tracks once a universal motivation can be established to transform the negative cultures we have created. (Refer to chapter entitled, Reversal of the underclass trend, when these concepts are dealt with in more depth).

At a personal level, the dispute with the neighbour, the rude boss, or the family upset, can all be 'healed' when positive reflection is introduced.

I proclaim that PS soul development encourages dialogue between ethnic and religious groups. Before resorting to conflict, kindlier words can be exchanged, and participants, who formerly were ready to take up arms, begin to reflect, 'But for the grace of God or Allah, could I be that very person whom I am facing with hate in my heart?

All such aspirations can enter the souls of young people to create a new generation of more caring people.

We have all been blessed with the means of finding our destiny, and each and everyone of us has a small part to play for the sake of the whole.

Caring people are happier people, and there can be no argument that the world needs PS.

The next chapter describes how it can be 'kick started' into activity.

POSITIVE SPIRIT - PROSPECTS FOR GROWTH

ALL MANNER of spiritual and ethical guidance has been 'fed into our souls" over the centuries, and although the providers frequently disagree about what is good for us, some positive traits of humanity are here to stay.

We now regard human rights, peace, compassion and justice as the future norm for a civilised world, but humanity is still very fragile, as the media bring to our notice on a regular basis.

We have not been motivated towards spirituality as we have been to technology, and it is the catching up process which is contained within the philosophy of Positive Spirit.

A starting point for PS, is the second that follows the placement of a newly born child in the arms of it's mother. At this point, the expression of joy, wonderment, and love, is conveyed from the soul of one adult to a new emerging one. A caring soul has entered the world joining millions of others, each with a potential to create a caring adult.

The philosophy behind PS is based on the belief that the caring element can be nurtured towards infinite growth, and once the philosophy has been shown to work, it will be carried forward with a self-generated enthusiasm.

The first barrier to cross is the myth that man is naturally wicked, and is out of control. This defeatist attitude needs reversing, and it requires a trend of optimism to set it on that path. The philosophy of PS provides that very thing with it's message, "we all have a little spark of God within us, and can help the world, each and every one of us, in our own little way!"

But the present shortcomings of humanity must be recognised and these can be short listed with greed, violence, hate and selfishness being the main ones. But supposing one traces back to the womb, every adult with these traits, can one possibly suggest that an infant is 'marked for wickedness' at birth?

Allowing for a small minority of children born with genes contain limiting factors, it is ridiculous to suppose that an infant has the stamp of a mugger, rapist, or drug pusher. Neither can one assume that a mother will give birth to a child with a caring and kindly character for life.

Every healthy child can become 'godly or devilish' by 'experience', not by hereditary factors or the 'mark of the devil'.

With human behaviour, it is a question of introducing holistic concepts into souls of children at a very early age, but the adult world, full of deep seated negative aspirations, requires a range of challenging soul building innovations.

The ultimate aim is to raise Positive Spirit consciousness so high, that concern for non-family is as sincere as that felt for one's nearest and dearest. I should remind the sceptics that the process is already under way, albeit in a haphazard manner not easily recognisable as spiritual progress.

A hundred years ago, wild life was still considered to exist largely for humankind to slaughter at will. But already, the young have a different concept about nature and express feelings of love and respect for wild animals. Even bull fighting will be banned before the next millenium.

We are mastering the primitive instinct for hunting and killing to feed our family. The remnants of this instinct are seen on the banks of rivers where fishermen 'brave' the hauling in of 'prey' on the end of a small hook. Country people still cling to their fox hunting, as a huge display in Hyde Park recently confirmed, but the trend of compassion is overwhelming and this so-called sport will be short-lived. The very idea of terrorising animals for our amusement will be abhorrent to the next generation

Today, few women dare to adorn themselves with animal furs. It is clear that animal rights are now big issues and the trend is towards caring and compassion in the animal world. However, it is sad to see militants distorting the kindness they are meant to portray by violence. They forget that humans are also animals, although not yet quite so endearing! But it is no wonder that passions are aroused about factory farmed animals, millions of which suffer behind the scenes in semi-darkness, out of mind and view of the general public, unaware of the cruelty involved for the sake of cheaper food. Again, there are pressure groups demanding the end to these barbaric practices.

One should remember that compassionate trends towards animal life have transpired within a hundred years, a flash of lightening in the annals of time.

Those sceptics who doubt whether our concern for wild animals can be extended to the 'tame' human variety, should dwell on UN troops being sent to rescue civilians from wars not of their choosing. Human rights and animal rights are now both global issues, albeit governments differ in their willingness to participate at this moment in time. But the trends for compassionate activities are there for all to see

The philosophy of PS aims to create an "inner impulse" to extend all such compassionate feelings to many issues which need holistic expression.

This will not be a revolution of the human soul but more of an evolution. Not to be confused with Darwin's biological approach.

Like the green movement before it, when spiritual truths dawn on people, souls start to blossom and when there is a realisation that each of us can contribute to a grand purpose of world transformation, the possibilities are exciting.

Souls can be compared to seedlings which need watering in a dry climate. Church, Synagogue and Mosque can provide some water for the shallow roots, but for the plants to blossom, they need an irrigation system to feed the root system. I believe that there is an inexhaustible supply of spiritual power to feed the roots, and that this supply of spiritual nourishment can be turned on by ourselves, and replenished instantly by God.

31

Part One

This concept of developing souls may be difficult to accept when we have been brought up to believe that spiritual self esteem is reserved for those in high places, however, if you look for spiritual trends and still fail to see any, I ask the following. What was the magic of Nelson Mandela when he arrived in the UK? He had been imprisoned and ill-treated for most of his adult life, yet he expressed forgiveness, peace, love and friendship to his former tormentors. His expression of sincerity crossed the barriers of colour and race and triggered the souls of millions.

At this moment in time, there are still conflicts to overcome, but trends for peace are here to stay. Charities have never been more active, and organisations such as Action Aid, Oxfam, Child Line, Help the Aged, the Samaritans, Save the Children, and numerous others, are unknowingly showing the direction mankind should be taking to further the spiritual evolution process. Numerous small compassionate groups of people volunteered to help alleviate suffering in Romania, Bosnia, Albania, and Chernobyl.

There is much to do, but an inexhaustible supply of 'soul power,' provided by the Almighty, is waiting for us to harness it!

Positive Spirit can be acquired by first realising that we have a spiritual base, irrespective of the 'warts' in our characters. The next step is to practice soul developing techniques which, because they are enjoyable, become self-fulfilling.

During this process, you find to your surprise that you are becoming a nicer person. Your friends and relatives notice it too! Will it be your imagination that they too are becoming nicer people? No, It will not be! Positive Spirit is positively catching, and it gradually squeezes out negative aspirations.

You will feel exhilarated that you are improving the world in your own very small way.

The philosophy of Positive Spirit is practical, optimistic, and catches on fast, from person to person, from group to group, from government to government, from country to country...It is a benign virus which can take over the world. If you still have doubts, just try out a few of the suggestions contained in the chapter headed, POSITIVE SPIRIT WORKING.

SCEPTICS GALORE

IT WAS UNIVERSALLY BELIEVED at one time that the world was flat and no one would dare to suggest otherwise until one could prove it otherwise. This attitude persists in our protective attitude to traditional beliefs.

Most people are only comfortable with things they understand, and the tendency is to treat new directions of belief as a threat.

To bring relief to those who see the PS philosophy in this light, I will emphasise that it involves the resurrection of something very old. Something which sages and prophets have been recommending for centuries, namely the 'universal harmony of the human spirit'. What is new, is the formulation of a plan to bring this into fruition.

When you have read this book, hopefully, you will see the key to the harmony which so many talk about, but assume it to be unattainable.

In the meantime, let me deal with some questions which sceptics are likely to raise.

Question One: "To think that a new kind of 'love thy neighbour' attitude can be introduced into the world when vast numbers of people are bent on exploiting and savaging each other, is ridiculous."

Reply: "Conflict is man made, and to state that so-called intelligent man will never be able to control and tame his aggressive instincts is an insult to those who have already made progress in that direction.

A hundred years ago, the very idea that the international community could agree to send their troops to the other end of the world to rescue civilians caught up in other peoples' wars, would have been dismissed out of hand.

There is now a concerted effort to protect human rights across the globe, and those who abuse them are now publicly exposed.

All these things have taken place in a flash of time relative to the progress of man from beast.

Everything points to a more compassionate and caring human evolving, more in keeping with the bond we all feel for those nearest and dearest to us.

Any ideas for speeding up the spiritual harmony of the human species must be welcome. The philosophy behind my PS concept is one of them."

Question Two: "Where is this enlightenment going to come from? Religious faiths have failed mankind along peaceful paths.

One only has to look at Christians murdering Moslems in Serbia, with the Mafia, drug barons, and extortionists, prospering regardless.

With all the power of religious dogma telling us to be good citizens, from Adam and Eve onwards, it must be naive to think that a Mr Nobody can come up with a prescription to save the world's souls."

Reply: "Your comments are expected. Indeed, I asked myself similar questions. How can a person with no special qualifications have the impertinence to come up with a philosophy for peace on Earth when 'specialists' versed in 'Godliness' are there for that very purpose?

My audacity is based on two criteria. Firstly our specialists, the religious faiths of the world, are in disarray themselves, and are not seen as a role model for universal camaraderie. Secondly, it is my firm belief that enthusiasm for caring, compassion, and goodwill has to come from within a person's soul 'pointing outwards', and one cannot effectively be taught these attributes 'from outside pointing in'.

If a child grows up with the notion that he or she has a responsibility to make the world a happier place, the soul will have been implanted with a seed of 'self esteem' which says, 'I am capable of doing a little job for mankind'.

Traditionally, we are taught that we are born sinful and that we must learn to fight wickedness to stem it's growth. In practice, this is counterproductive because man's ego is always rebellious. In contrast, self-generated caring attributes are more likely to enter the soul bank and be a credit to humanity.

Whilst 'soul implants' in childhood are the most promising route to PS awareness, we adults have the means to raise our 'soul levels', by first being aware that we can do so, and then surprisingly find a hankering to do something about it. This is not a fantasy! Thousands of people already get this urge. It may be nurses, health workers, or volunteers who help the ill, the handicapped, or the homeless.

Your question was. Where is all this enlightenment going to come from? It will come from you and me, and in due course, a billion like-minded people. They will get the inspiration from a feeling of wanting to help humanity in his or her lifetime."

Question Three: "Why can't you use the Christian religion as a vehicle for promoting man's salvation.? After all, love, compassion, and goodwill are the basics of Christian teaching, and Positive Spirit seems to be one and the same thing. There are so many cults, sects and unorthodox faiths, that no wonder people are confused. Your philosophy seems likely to add to the confusion, which might result in people forsaking religious faith altogether."

Reply: "There are similarities between PS thinking and Christian ethics, and indeed the philosophy of PS can work through Christianity and be responsible for bringing more of the teachings of Jesus to fruition.

But the PS philosophy is inter-racial, inter-religious, and free of dogma. It is not a religion or a cult. It is a way of holistic thinking and living. In this respect, it can prosper with all faiths co-operating.

One must face it, whilst religious faith has been instrumental in creating much of the goodness in mankind, it has also caused immense suffering in the process. Persecutions and holocausts have largely been carried out by so-called Christians. All these things are not the fault of Christianity or other religions: they just happen in spite of them. It is a case of souls not being strong enough to live by the ethics they are meant to represent.

Godliness is within the souls of all people, of all faiths and all cultures, and it is raising the level of universal caring and compassion which is the issue. I feel Jesus would have gone along with that wholeheartedly."

Question Four: "I think your philosophy is based on wishful thinking in the face of uncompromising reality.

The human character has an inborn barbarity within it. It is greedy, selfish, and aggressive, and to have ideas for changing the human race along the lines of the Positive Spirit philosophy, is a dream founded on extreme optimism."

Reply: "Your statement exactly portrays the low self-esteem which we hold about ourselves, and seems to suggest our minds have been taken over by a devilish fiend, over whom we have no control.

Let me enlighten you, the greedy, selfish and aggressive human, you describe, is of our own making, and there is no logical reason to suppose that 'soul enhancement' at an early age cannot play an important part in eliminating this trait within a few generations.

But adults, too, can be inspired to show compassion and honesty on a grand scale if we put our minds to it. The worst person has some good in him and if this is cultivated, the yoke of unpleasantness can all but disappear.

One of many ideas is to make a challenge of intent across the world's TV network and Internet. It challenges every nation to contribute 10% of their youth to a voluntary peace-action-force, specifically designed to alleviate poverty and rout out drug addiction.

As I write these words, a news flash announces that a group called the Halo Trust has been formed, which involves volunteers going to minefields to remove land mines which have continued to blow off legs of people trying to farm their land.

I hope I may have convinced you that the philosophy of Positive Spirit is not just one more "talking shop".

But replying to your comment about wishful thinking. Optimism is the embryo of creativity, and if we 'wishfully think' that Positive Spirit will spread peace and harmony across the world, people will be inspired to take up the challenge!"

NOT A FANTASY!

IF WE HAVE THE INTELLIGENCE to send people to the moon, and the ability to put the Bible on a micro-chip, we must surely have the means of making ourselves more kindly and balanced. But intellect and soul are separate entities, and bringing the latter to guide the former along holistic lines continues to cause immense problems for the human race.

People in power so often make unethical or inconsiderate decisions for expediency or profit when holistic considerations take second place.

The key requirement is to increase the spiritual, divine, content of souls, so they can become more dominant in all our thinking and decision making.

Firstly, there must be a recognition that ordinary people can generate Divine Power, which I call Positive Spirit. This includes those who do not consider themselves very moral and law abiding. Even criminals have soul development potential. But to generate more Positive Spirit, it is enlightening to see how it has developed and where the shortfall exists.

Our justice system, and attempts to establish love and harmony have all arisen from active souls, often sparked by ideals inspired by philosophers, theologians and prophets.

Many thousands of people are already expressing their spirituality by taking up caring activities, exemplified by people in the nursing profession, social workers and those who have chosen to help the homeless, the abused and the poverty stricken.

There is something in common between those who volunteer to nurse the sick in remote parts of Africa and the Samaritans who try to talk people out of suicide. They all hear an 'inner voice' which says 'go and help'. This is their 'soul power' directing their thinking and actions.

The replication of this power so Positive Spirit can spread from one end of the world to the other, is no fantasy. Indeed, the groundwork for PS enlargement has been prepared by the green movement with a new-found love for the natural world. The escalation of these trends to cover humanity, is predictable.

My optimism is based on observation that we all enthusiastic about things which give us maximum fulfilment, and spiritual achievements of the caring variety are something very special and exciting. This is supported by personal contact with people involved in convoying aid to Romania, Bosnia and Chernobyl.

A recent poll in the UK and USA confirms a trend of disillusionment about the notion that wealth brings happiness. High income is now seen not to bring high contentment and people are searching for more rewarding outlets for their existence. A new word has been coined, namely "downshifting", which means a shifting down of life's perceived priorities. In effect, this means that there is a self-inspired wish to relegate materialistic and often selfish values in favour of something more rewarding. This denotes that values of a more selfless and spiritual nature are already sown by the 'light workers of the world' and we are seeing a more enlightened human being on the horizon, one which is asking, "What is the true purpose of my life?"

I am confident that the level of spirituality a hundred years from now, will be a dominant feature of humanity, with each generation passing it to the next in an almost instinctive way.

No! Positive Spirit is not a fantasy, and the more you study the philosophy for it's growth, your soul will be nudging you to become involved in some way or other.

CHANGING HISTORY

HISTORY BOOKS CAN DISTORT facts because opinions within them are biased in favour of the people who read them. For instance, in China, the British claim pride in that they brought trade to that country, whilst the Chinese say they they introduced Opium to exploit them.

Therefore, in posing the following question, one should select a trusted and respected international historian, "What can the young generation do to avoid the mistakes so carefully recorded in history?"

Ah, he will say, "I merely record what man has been up to. Please refer to psychologists, theologians, and sociologists about these matters."

This sums up the folly of specialisation. The past is separated from both the present and the future, as though they were all unrelated aspects.

The purpose of education, which should be the manifestation of wisdom, is lost in a bottomless pit of separate statistics. Furthermore, if you do not teach history with a purposeful aim to bring wisdom into the future, the urge to improve a grossly imperfect world, is sterile. One can see the reflection of this omission in government circles, when planning ahead is confined to a political party's term in office.

Let us state the ultimate aims for a new enlightened era. It must be for men and women to live in harmony with each other across the world, create universal justice, and feel a camaraderie for each other irrespective of ethnic origin, race, religion or colour.

Being an optimist about man's spiritual future, I project an extract from a feature in the Times newspaper of January 2050 AD :-

'History has already recorded, since the start of the new millennium, a new era of international camaraderie. One benefit of modern technology are the three dimensional screen images which are now available even to the very poor. Scenes now portray vividly those suffering from starvation, oppression and deprivation, just as though one's own close family were involved. The trauma of earthquake victims are now felt in one's own living room, so strikingly realistic are the visions.'

The above is a realistic prediction, but technology rarely feeds the soul in this manner. On the contrary, it's progress is usually at the expense of the soul, which should really be in the driving seat.

However soul development and compassion are complimentary to each other, and seeing suffering so vividly, will, without doubt, stimulate the international caring element. Voluntary service will become more universal and part of life's fulfilment.

It has been said that seeing too much suffering can make us immune to compassion. This is a confusion between emotion and the caring element. Nurses see suffering every hour of the day, but they still care for their patients, and some live in discomfort far from home and obtain fulfilment from their deserving work.

Looking at historical oversights, the most glaring one is the omission of 'soul education', without which mankind cannot prosper.

One positive step involves an holistic subject being brought into the teaching syllabus. Children must be aware that one reason for being given life is to improve the life of others. At the present time, this concept is largely sterile because the 'taking' element rather than the 'giving' one, has become the norm of life's motivation in a materialistic world. But this outlook can be reversed even within a decade or two.

The PS philosophy inspires us to search our hearts for ways of making the world a happier place. Numerous avenues will bring such positive ideas into reality. Often individual people with holistic aspirations can generate positive ideas which others take up and expand. Leading the way, will be spiritual and interfaith groups, charities, and caring agencies. But most important, international holistic education, introduced early in childhood, will be the key to a peaceful and just world in the centuries to follow.

The United Nations will see all these movements as complimentary to their own efforts in achieving world stability and peace. At this moment of time, offshoots of the UN already give support to any group or organisation which inspire harmony of mind, body and spirit.

When we talk of changing the course of history we should be including changes in our daily activities, because 'soul enhancing' ideas can be slipped into the habits of a lifetime in a most enjoyable way.

Soul activation. First let us list a few simple activities which, rightly or wrongly, Western culture has taught us to do 'naturally' without emotion. If we are lucky to have a home and a job to go to, the following ritual is typical:

If we are a man, we wash, shave, dress, and have breakfast.

If we have a car, we drive it in accordance with the rules of the road, and having reached our destination, park our car in a space provided, and enter our place of work. We greet our fellow workers and settle down to fulfil our employment.

Whilst emotive incidents may have occurred during this daily routine, we have happily volunteered to follow a conventional pattern. We are relaxed about it, and would feel uncomfortable to be different from our peers.

But in the quest for being 'comfortable', there is no reason why we cannot introduce holistic aspirations into our daily routine. For instance, before you leave for work, you pop in next door to see if that lonely old lady is all right. On the way to work, you are really courteous to other drivers, whether they deserve it or not. When you get to work, you give a cheery greeting to that 'different' person who cannot speak English very well and looks rather vulnerable.

Hotel managers are instructed in a parrot-wise manner to say "Have a nice day" to tourists, so as to make a good impression, but the comment becomes irrelevant to both giver and receiver.

However, if a sincere warm welcome is to be portrayed to the foreigner, then genuine it must be. Goodwill is created from the soul not from a book on etiquette. How is this done?

The learning curve of our hotel manager needs to take an holistic direction. It would be helpful if he could imagine that he is a foreigner in a strange land, feeling tired and rather lonely. He then has to ask himself, "What greeting would make me feel welcome and comfortable if the role was reversed?"

By putting him in the shoes of the foreigner, he now genuinely greets him from his heart, and this is portrayed in the tone and manner of speech. From now on, when he greets people, his soul is more in control. He has become a nicer person and he feels good about it, because the reflection of

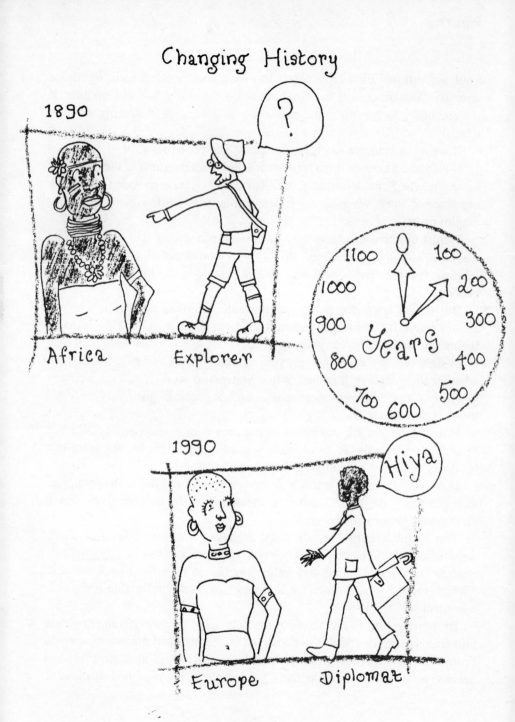

goodwill from the happy foreigner has "bounced back at him. He has become a goodwill creator.

The above event is obviously a minuscule example of Positive Spirit activity but goodwill creation can so easily become a natural expanding trait of the human race because it is enjoyable, and bounces from one person to another, chain letter style.

The Positive Spirit philosophy holds the key to exploiting this trend and 'changing history' for the better.

SQUEEZING THE EVIL OUT

THERE ARE THOSE who predict an apocalypse for mankind, and whenever humanity appears out of control, statements about the end of the world arise regularly. It appears that such predictions are based on ancient writings, massaged to comply with the belief that the evils of mankind are unstoppable. This is reflected in some American films which portray futuristic scenes of brutality amongst disintegrating cities and chaos.

This is pessimism at it's most destructive, because if you talk yourself into doom, that will be the outcome. Conversely, optimism yields positive horizons which in turn yield hope and expectations. These are the embryos of resolve and positive achievements.

Yes, there is greed, violence and injustice but we know from history that they result from false values, and social instability. These evils can become 'fossils of an earlier age' by the end of the 21st century if the reasons for their creation are studied in depth.

The official line is that we are basically sinful, and that we should be fighting the evil within ourselves by taking regular spoonfuls of 'purging medicine' to dispel evil trends. This negative message for our souls creates a low self-worthiness. It builds a subconscious resentment, like being found guilty for a crime not yet committed.

It also allows hypocrisy to fester in those who express sin as the prime trait in humankind. I was reminded of this vividly in my early years at a private school when the headmaster read sermons in the school chapel but

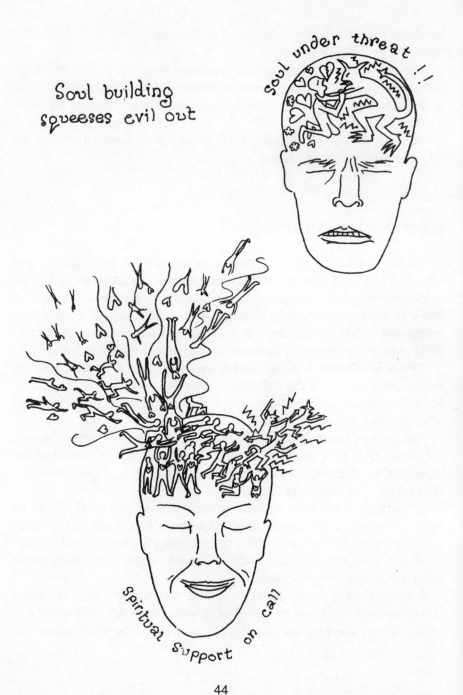

Soul building
squeeses evil out

Soul under threat !!!

Spiritual Support on Call

took a delight in mercilessly beating the 'sin out of children'. His delight in bringing fear into the class room and swaggering in with his cane, could well be explained by a religious belief that he was fulfilling a driving-out-of-sin operation. In truth, he was sowing the seed of bullying, perversion and negative attitudes in his charges. Those children without loving parents to counter the 'soul damage' inflicted, could well be replicas of the person responsible for the damage. It would not be out of place to relate the behaviour of other 'ruthless masters' on the world scene to similar childhood experiences.

The concept that 'the devil in us' dominates humankind, encourages the very evils which the 'medicine' is trying to remove. This is an outmoded notion and needs 'standing on its head' and reversing. In effect, we should start from scratch with the concept that every person has a 'goodness base' which will blossom if encouraged to grow from within. This does not mean that discipline should be abandoned in child rearing but it should be fairly applied in an atmosphere of 'these are the rules for living, and we abide by them for the good of us all'.

The soul-development potential I refer to, is not a privileged gift for any particular social group. Indeed, primitive tribes often display more sensitivity and generosity than their 'civilised' counterparts who disregard ethics at a stroke.

A person originating from the Brazilian rain forest, is likely to display the same character trends as one born in the Western hemisphere, when brought up 'on a level playing field'. It is all a question of education, the term being used in the widest sense.

But people are born with dominant or passive personalities. If a man grows to be dishonest, he may be a 'passive' thief and steal quietly and perhaps cunningly, whilst a 'dominant' one may be the leader of a gang, and resort to violence. But there is no question of being born a criminal.

All people have elements of both feminine and masculine but passive people are inclined to be gentle, artistic, musical, and intuitive, whilst dominant ones are inclined to be vigorous, power hungry, and achievers with a 'get up and go' mentality for better or for worse. History shows how this opportunist group have created immense problems for the human race, and to this day we see the lack of spiritual intuition preventing our handling technology with holistic wisdom.

But both of above groups thrive on Positive Spirit, the substance which gives harmony and meaning to our lives.

A gentle person may be more likely to show loving care for people, perhaps by comforting and counselling the distressed, whilst a vigorous person might choose to join a mountain rescue team or a lifeboat crew.

You may well enquire how concern of one person for another, can really become so universal. Here is a true story which gives a clue to the source of soul growth which is the very essence of spiritual growth.

During the last war, a Japanese soldier was interrogating a British prisoner, and using torture to gain vital information. In terrible pain, the prisoner shouted "Mother, help me, help me!" whereupon the soldier stopped the proceedings and made excuses to his superior that the prisoner had no useful information to offer. It was twenty years later that he explained why he had disobeyed his orders, 'When I was a young boy I hurt my foot badly and I shrieked for my mother to help me. The British prisoner had shouted the same words. This had jolted my soul, and I felt the pain he was suffering. I then knew what I was doing was wrong, so I stopped". This Japanese man, now elderly, regularly visits a shrine for war dead, and prays for forgiveness for the misdeeds he perpetrated during the war.

We can see from this story that the potential for souls to squeeze out evil, is not a glib fanciful thought, but something very real indeed.

The philosophy behind Positive Spirit will build up a natural and strong revulsion to cruelty, so that no self respecting soldier would dream of practising it, even when provoked.

The solution for bringing souls up to strength, is to stress from the cradle that the purpose of being brought into this wonderful world, is to play a part in making it a kindlier place in which to live.

If this can become a priority in our concept for being given life, evils can be prevented from maturing, and those that squeeze through the net will wither in a New Coming Age of justice and compassion.

THE CHILDHOOD EFFECTS

'WHEN THE PENNY HAS DROPPED' about the potential of children to 'heal the world', we shall be wondering why our intelligence has taken us a few millennia to come to that conclusion.

We can tune our communication through satellites in space but when it comes to 'tuning the soul', we founder miserably. Religious and democratic institutions try their best to guide us along holistic lines, but constantly we search for solutions from the wrong end of the spectrum.

The basic faults are twofold. Firstly, there is a low priority for tackling the actual causes of problems and an almost total lack of forward planning to eradicate them. It happens in the home and in the high street. It appears in government circles and on an international level.

Negative 'Child Effects'

The idea that the ills of the world displayed in the media, can be healed by children sounds naive and rather ridiculous on the face of it. But the 'chicken and egg' situation should be studied in more depth.

It is well known that children within a family lacking kindness, love and consideration for others, will perpetuate the same negative traits.
Bullies in the school playground are ripe to become muggers higher up the scale. The 'home education' has ensnared it in a negative attitude towards other members of the human race.

Playing soldiers has traditionally been fun for young children. They are excited at identifying themselves with the power to destroy an imaginary enemy but we make no effort to convey the terrible effect modern weapons have on those at the receiving end. Indeed, the establishment convey to the child that such weapons are a normal feature of mankind and pacifism is rather a wimpish concept. In the USA, the possession of a gun portrays a ' macho cowboy' image and becomes almost a status symbol for many young adolescents.

Neutral 'Child Effects'

On a lighter note, playing trains is something we have all enjoyed as a child and the love for it comes right through into the world of adult hobbies.

The Childhood Effect

Playing trains

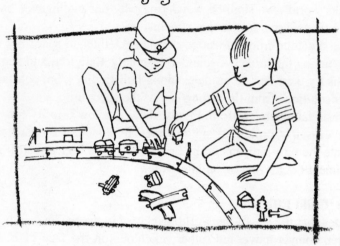

Still playing trains

Thousands of lofts are filled with models of trains realistically produced in miniature. Magazines on the subject proliferate.

It is clear that a happy 'childhood effect' has enabled thousands of people to 'lose themselves' in the delights of their early life. Apart from perhaps soothing a stressful life, one might assume that the 'train loft' syndrome serves no useful purpose to mankind, but it has a vital significance. What it does, is to show that enjoyments and fascinations of childhood pass through the adolescence period and influence the thought patterns in adulthood What if 'world healing' enjoyments could become part of children's horizons? Youngsters are already enthralled with the animal kingdom. The possibilities are mind boggling!

Positive 'Child Effects'

We have seen how seriously 'home education' can affect the attitudes and aspirations of the growing child, but since we are also faced with 're-educating the educators', one might suppose we have an impossible task. Not so!

The clue for optimism appeared in a leading newspaper. For an experiment, children were allowed to interview teachers for their suitability to teach them. Astonishingly, their requirements for a good teacher were full of wisdom. They chose teachers who would make lessons interesting, be disciplinarians when necessary but have a sense of humour. Let us carry this one stage further.

Children are taught to be honest, unselfish and kind but they soon find their elders are hypocrites once they face the real world of 'everyone for himself'. It explains much of the lack of respect the younger generation have for their elders. The question therefore arises as to whether children can point to their elders that they are 'making a mess of the world' and that things could improve by their so doing. On the face of it, this idea sounds grossly improbable, but there is a dimension of the 'child effect' which has not been exploited.

If children are taught that part of their purpose in life when they grow up is to reverse the shortcomings of the human race, a vibrant self worthiness is created. Like the current movement for saving endangered animal species, a torch to help the human species is born. Ways to 'improve the world'

The Childhood Effect

Playing war

Real war

would be a challenge to young adolescents. Their horizons would be switched from *'what's in it for me'* to *'what's in it for them'*.

Now is the time to switch some of the passion for the 3 Rs in education to a curriculum for living, when young people can find an enjoyment comes from 'giving' rather than just 'taking'.

The victims of injustice, poverty, and natural disasters are 'waiting' for a crusade of young such people to come to their rescue. The realisation by the younger generation that they have a job to do, cannot come too soon. In the next chapter, entitled Peace Child, you will find that a section of the young world community have already woken up to such responsibilities.

PEACE CHILD

GROWN-UPS have not made a very good job of looking after our planet and this has given rise to a strange situation because we now need to listen to our children for holistic guidance, whereas wisdom was meant to be the domain of adults!

Is it not their right to be consulted and express their views for they are the ones who suffer from inherited pollutions and misdeeds of their elders?

Children's minds are not cluttered with motives of power politics and commercial gain, so their ideas for a peaceful world could well contain holistic wisdoms which we ignore at our peril.

In our ego-centred world, our wisdom does not necessarily come with age, and the time has come to give the world's young people a degree of responsibility for the world's future, something that hitherto has been left entirely to adults with disastrous results.

In one short sentence, Peace Child is about giving today's children the confidence to create a better tomorrow! But how can this be done?

There is one organisation very much active in this area. It is called Peace Child International, which was founded in 1981. It's purpose was to give children a voice in world affairs and thus stimulate an inner expression of confidence in children's minds and souls, which said, 'I can play a part in making the world a better and happier place'.

With the support of UN agencies, enthusiasm for peaceful expression is created in a number of ways.

One idea was to stage a musical play in which children from every country were invited to participate. The story is set in the future when the people of the world are living in peace with one another and with their environment. Young people were challenged to think what they had done with their lives to create that peaceful existence and invited to bring their ideas into the structure of the play.

The growth of Peace Child from it's early concept has been dramatic. Children, mainly between the ages of 7 and 17 years have organised meetings and conferences on a variety of subjects, including world peace, the environment, human rights, and international understanding.

In the year 1995, it produced a Children's History of the United Nations, having earlier produced a handbook entitled, 'Children's state of the planet'.

What is so encouraging is that the enthusiasm for peaceful initiatives by young people now shame many delegates at the United Nations who are inclined to drag their feet on peaceful initiatives so as to gain some advantage for their country by doing so. In effect, children are stimulating peaceful gestures which their elders cannot ignore. They are without doubt, in a subtle way, 'nudging world peace at source.'

The following extracts from an address at the Earth Summit, June 1992 by a 12 year old girl, Severn Suzuki, sum up the aspirations of Peace Children,

"Hello, I am Severn Suzuki, speaking for the Environmental Children's Organisation.

We are a group of 12 to 13 year old children who have travelled 6000 miles to tell you adults that you must change your ways.

I am here to speak for all generations to come.

I am here to speak for the starving children around the world whose cries you cannot hear.

I am here to speak for the suffering of children, through stupid wars which were not of our doing.

Peace Child - Earth Summit 92

Part One

I am here to speak for dying animals who have nowhere else to go.

I do not have all the solutions, but when you make holes in the ozone layers, burn down precious forests, and make deserts where things grew before, I know who make the problems.

At this meeting, you may be delegates of your governments, business people, reporters, or politicians, but in reality you are mothers and fathers, brothers and sisters, aunts and uncles. You are all somebody else's child!

I am only a child, but I know I am part of one big human family, five billion strong. We all share the same air, water, land, and soil of the planet.

So we are all in this together and should act as one single group towards one single goal.

I am only a child yet I know that if all the money spent on war was used to end poverty, injustice and improve the environment, what a wonderful place this earth would be.

At school, even in our kindergarten, you teach us to behave. You tell us:-
not to fight with others,
to always respect people,
to clean up our mess,
not to hurt other creatures,
to share and not be greedy.
Then why do you do the very things which you tell us not to do ?

Well, all the things you do make us cry at night. You grown-ups say you love us, but on behalf of all the children in the world, I challenge you, please make your actions reflect your words.

Thank you for listening."

Note. Peace Child International works with several United Nations agencies to promote UN initiatives in which young people can become involved. (Address at end of book)

'Peace Child is about giving today's children the confidence to create a better tomorrow.'

POSITIVE SPIRIT HEALS

POSITIVE SPIRIT IS A TWO-WAY THING. If you develop your PS powers which I have shown is ,perfectly feasible, you release these vibrations wherever you go and impart them to those you meet in your day to day activities. It comes naturally after a while.

But imagine now you are a different person, one that is stressed with everything in life appearing to have gone wrong. You have lost a dear one and in your grief your work has suffered and you have become redundant. You are deeply depressed and life has become meaningless. You search for a reason for living.

One day you go to a friend's house, and there is a person you meet there who 'radiates' happiness. It is irritating at first, but after chatting for a while, you find yourself 'coming out of your mood', and find temporary enjoyment.

You confide in that person your problems and wonder why you feel so much better having done so, because having returned home, you now decide to snap out of it, and do something positive with your life. Life is good after all!

The above hypothetical situation might seem to rest solely in the area of psychology, but there is a spiritual element, because once the 'soul enhancing' process has been 'kick-started', those who have adopted the PS philosophy are healers without realising it.

That person on the verge of suicide, has received some gentle verbal encouragement but you will have imparted 'positive healing' quite out of proportion to the spoken words, because you will have been 'exuding' the same wonderful quality to the patient. Albeit, you will not be aware of the healing process.

The idea of becoming a 'miracle worker' should not go to one's head. Most people have the power of drawing in Positive Spirit and 'exhaling' it for the benefit of others as well as gaining real happiness for oneself in the process.

But the 'self awareness' enhancement of Positive Spirit is still in its infancy, because the idea of DIY spirituality is anathema to those with rigid entrenched religious views.

Let us all agree on one thing, Positive Spirit has been around for an eternity and if peace, love and universal understanding can flourish by spiritual enhancement, albeit, by unusual means, who would wish to block such a worthy evolutionary process?

POSITIVE THINKING PLUS

THERE IS a superb book by Norman Vincent Peal entitled the Power of Positive Thinking, which has sold over fifteen million copies. One must ask oneself, what motivates such vast numbers of people to buy a book on the subject of thinking positively?

After reading the first chapter or two, the reason comes to light. In this competitive world, when millions of people are trying to get ahead of their contemporaries to reach the 'treasures' of materialism, and when the yardstick of success is chosen by high performance in the workplace, millions find it difficult to make it! If they could reach the performance of the winners, the yardstick standard would be raised, creating a higher hurdle for those who now become losers, so there is a ready market for his book.

People who have a low respect for themselves are pessimistic and unhappy. Mr Peale's book helps to reverse those feelings, and that must be part of it's appeal. He describes numerous ways of boosting optimism, ones self-respect, one's ego, and one's capability to do anything, if one sets one's mind to it. It does a great job in giving encouragement to those at the end of their tether, such as the unemployable, the poverty stricken, the feeble minded, and those who, for some reason, have lost confidence in themselves, perhaps through family breakdown or illness.

He often mentions how faith in God helps in the process of trying to get there and how prayer can work wonders to achieve the goals we set ourselves. This is so very true. But it is the interpretation of 'trying to get there', which worries me a bit, for I believe we often set the wrong standards for so called success.

People who learn to boost their will power by thinking positively may acquire their version of success at the expense of someone else, who then searches for positive means of retrieving his lost self worthiness. It can become a vicious circle. We cannot all be 'winners'.

Here is a hypothetical situation in the workplace. A person is trying hard to reach a manager's position by adopting an aggressive stance to obtain respect. He reads how to be firm, positive and confident, and he obtains his position with the former manager now being his underling. Unless he befriends the displaced manager, and makes him feel good in some way, one negative situation has been replaced with a similar one.

You see, there is a missing ingredient in the motivation process! Unless thoughts are positive from an ethical and kindly point of view, positive thinking has limited value. In a nut shell, it is a question of whether the goal is to think positively or positively think. There is a subtle difference.

Even bringing God into positive thinking, needs careful evaluation. Soldiers of every conceivable denomination pray to their God to see them through to victory. If they are on opposite sides, they should dwell on whether their war is just or not, before calling on their God for positive help. But one should question the interpretation of courage when one faces another human with killing in mind. Are we being dehumanised? What of the family of that person who will be devastated? This raises a further fundamental question. Should our souls be manipulated to kill another human being?

The positive thinkers should be asking themselves when they use that newly attained confidence, am I creating any unkind situations for others to endure? Am I going to be a better person following my achievement? Can I do something worthwhile for the world with my positive thoughts?.

Mr Peale's book does an admirable job in many ways, because it raises people's self esteem and enables them to cope with the pressures of modern life. But some of the goals in life are 'sick' and positive thoughts need realigning to cope with the soul destroying elements we mistakenly value as success.

People who classify themselves as positive thinkers and who have no need for a book to tell them be more positive, can well be the very ones who should be more holistic in their 'positiveness'. At present, we are in a period of callous competitive thinking, based on selfishness. But I am very confident that this trend can be reversed with Positive Spiritual Thinking!

THINK AND REFLECT

* When we are born, our differences are only cosmetic. Culture, status, religion and ideology are thrust on us and divide us, but these things are 'man made' and what we can divide, we can unite!

* There are vast amounts of Godly people longing for fraternity. They just need to meet and tell each other!

* There is a magic formula for resolving conflicts. It is this. Seek a spiritual objective to resolve the conflict rather than one based on gain.

* How nice it would be if the year 2000 witnessed all religious groups joyously accepting that we are all of one family in the eyes of a Godhead.

* Caring, compassion and love are sown in the hugs of a mother grasping her newly born. The spiritual seedlings from these are the creators of nicer grown-ups.

❋ God has brought us into this world to enjoy the fruits of living. Should we not say, 'thank you', and put something back into it, so as to make it just that little bit better than when we found it?

❋ When Arabs, Christians, Hindus, Jews, and Moslems can hug each other and say, "We are brothers", and mean it, then there is a light within the tunnel rather than at the end of it !

❋ In the quest to impart knowledge and literacy to our children, we have overlooked a prime need, namely, the teaching of caring, compassion and universal brotherhood.

❋ Religious dogma is politics in a spiritual overcoat. It offers us advice for our weaknesses and our excesses, but does little to build up our own spirituality to handle them.

❋ If you receive hate, your heart will breed the very same negative feeling, Cultivate love and it will catch on fast and heal the hate!

❋ We are part of something bigger than ourselves, and we should not be shy in reminding ourselves when power and possessions seem to take over our reason for being here!

❋ A self-challenging thought is, 'If the world followed me, would it be a better place?'

❋ When you do a kind deed with no advantage to yourself, your spirit is going positive and your soul abounds with exhilaration. Just try it and see for yourself. It works every time!

PART TWO

POSITIVE SPIRIT WORKING

POSITIVE BEDTIME THINKING

Before you nod off into dreamland, try an experiment.

Clear your mind of problems and say to yourself in a positive manner, "I can **will** the following to happen and it will happen"

Then demand of yourself, "Tomorrow, I shall wake up feeling that life is good and this feeling will saturate my home."

Follow on with, "I shall be calm and capable of handling problems around me in a peaceful manner."

Don't doubt about your ability to succeed in this experiment!

We all have the power to work mini-miracles.

It is just about tuning in to the spiritual wavelength that the almighty has provided us with, and using it!

Part Two

THE 'DIANA EFFECT'

WHEN THE NEWS of Princess Diana's death reached the world, millions were brought to tears.

Why was she so loved?

It was because we identified her life and problems with some of our own. She was 'one of us'. Her fallibilities were ones we recognised within ourselves.

But it was her caring and compassionate work with the sick and suffering, which struck a chord in the hearts of us all. She was the person we would like to be, and her humanity struck a note with our own caring aspirations, which we are usually too busy to express ourselves.

In effect she became our proxy for the good deeds we fantasise about, but don't get round to doing anything about them.

The explosion of affection across the world, I predict, will be known as the 'Diana Effect' because she has highlighted what lies dormant in the human race, a genuine desire to contribute to a more compassionate world.

NOT SO 'DIFFERENT' PEOPLE

WHEN FIRST MEETING A PERSON with a different colour, creed, or race, there is a feeling of discomfort at first, even distrust.

This feeling is a knee jerk animal instinct which says, "Look out, he's not one of us". But we should positively welcome someone a little different, and put ourselves 'in the shoes' of that different person.

Just stop and dwell on the fact. If God had decided you would be born to a Nigerian, a Pigmy or a Chinaman, you would be looking at pale faces with some astonishment at their 'unhealthy' complexions. We are all of one race, the human race, with only a few cosmetic variations.

ACTION. Be the first person to show a hand of friendship to that 'different' person, who feels a little lost and intimidated. Your greeting will be noted, and passed back to the country of origin, and thus you will have sowed the seed of universal friendship. A small start that can snowball across the globe.

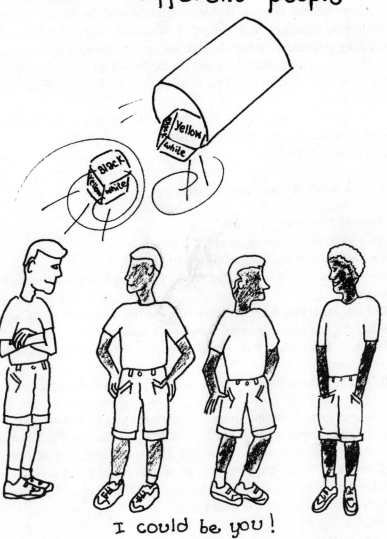

Part Two

BE HAPPY, DON'T WORRY, BE FRIENDLY!

IT IS CLAIMED that one in four of us suffer from stress, depression or mental disorders, yet few are deprived of basic conventional needs.

Some believe that our problems centre round the urban style existence we live in, separated from the peace of natural surroundings which have a soothing influence. Others believe we are obsessed by the material things in life, so much so, that we cannot see the 'wood for the trees', but whatever the cause, self-created ills of the mind can usually be cured with some useful 'know how'.

It requires a mix of self-counselling and common-sense, bound together with a spiritual concept, which urges your inner self to see the good in everyone and yourself.

You ask yourself some questions, such as :-

What do I really enjoy in life?
What gives you peace of mind?
Are you short of food, a bed, or a roof?
Do you 'feel good' about Nelson Mandela and the peacemakers of this world?
Did you know that by being given life, you are important to the world?
When did you last let go and 'laugh your head off?'
Did you know that less wealthy people are happier than those with 'everything?'
When did you last tell the ones nearest to you heart that you love them?

Your replies to these questions will not give you an instant cure, but your soul will give you a nudge about what really matters in life. You will begin to think what nonsense it is to get upset and depressed at really minor problems, you will begin to see the best in people, and they will see the difference in you. Your sense of humour will increase and laughter will heal those around who seem unhappy.

There is a nice saying:-

'A shared joy doubles the joy. A shared sorrow halves the sorrow'

Are you already feeling on top of the world? Not yet? But work on it!

The joy of seeing what's good in the world rather than just the 'warts', is exhilarating. Soon everybody will be doing it!

Newspaper editors, please get this message.

Part Two

HARMLESS EXCITEMENT

IN REAL LIFE, most of us feel comfortable to be civil and calm, but a throw back to our primitive and often violent past is fantasised on our television screens. In this way, excitement and violence is obtained in a secure home environment without having to experience the frightening truth of it.

But when young people are raised in a deprived or hostile environment of an inner city, they tend to get hooked on the macho roles of the characters on the 'box' and act out the parts in real life. This is reflected in hooliganism, petty crime and drug abuse.

We can prevent such trends if harmless forms of excitement can be introduced to steer youngsters away from the damaging ones. There are even 'excitements' of an achieving nature which are character building, because they provide something which everyone needs, and that is self-respect.

Action. Support organisations in the community which offer young people challenging activities which are positive. Conventional sports activities are good, but not always exciting enough. Let us look at some challenging pastimes for youngsters and compare them with some of the negative ones they may be following at the present time.

POSITIVE	NEGATIVE
Hang gliding	Vandalism
Rock climbing	Racial attacks
Go karting	Mugging
Canoeing	Joy riding
Wind Surfing	Bullying
Motor bike rallies	Shop lifting
Stock car racing	Gang warfare
Pony trekking	Hooliganism
Adventure holidays	Drug taking

Note. The subject of this chapter is dealt with in detail within the chapter entitled, 'Reversing the underclass trend'.

BEING A PARENT

BRINGING UP CHILDREN is a tricky business these days, and it would be nonsense to try and cram all there is to know in a few lines. On the contrary, I am advising you to study the issue in depth on the day you find there is a little one on the way.

If one wishes to play the piano, one doesn't press the keyboard haphazardly and hope a nice tune comes out.

If one aims to be a chef, there is a craft in selecting the right ingredients, and cooking them correctly. Few would chance making up one's recipe as one goes along and expecting the end product to be edible.

We go to school, and possibly university, to study a range of subjects to bring success and happiness into our lives, but there is one huge omission. The most important subject of all, namely bringing up a family, is left to nature, just as though we were birds, mice or monkeys in the wild.

We are all living in a hectic modern world and our children are faced with a mass of negative distractions making it increasingly difficult for both parents and teachers to handle.

To the point of this chapter.

All of us mothers and fathers, whether we are from a lower income group or ones in the top bracket, should not be too proud to take courses in parenting. If these are not yet available we should press for their introduction without delay.

Could we not introduce the subject of parenting into the school curriculum? There can be no more important a subject than the bringing up children to become well balanced, thoughtful and wise members of the human race. The world needs plenty of them!

Note. Several addresses about the subject of parenting are listed in the index.

Part Two

COURTESY IS CATCHING

ONE CAN TEACH ONESELF to be courteous in the most unlikely circumstances, and it can be rather rewarding.

It goes like this. All people who are rude, discourteous,or unpleasant, have some background reason for being so disagreeable.

They are unhappy and frustrated people. They are 'getting their own back' by releasing pent-up feelings in unacceptable ways.

Lets take the road hog, who finds he can let lose his anger by intimidating other road users with his weapon, his car.

To be nice to such people might seem unnatural. You might be called a wimp in the bargain, but endure it.

What then do you say to this road hog when you meet him at the traffic lights? How about, 'please do calm down!. You seem very upset this morning. Hope you feel better soon. Life is not that bad you know'.

You would get a funny look, and he might think you were being sarcastic. On the other hand, you may have sown a seed of rationality and harmony in that person, so that he could handle his problems without aggravating those not responsible for his demise.

If you had allowed yourself to get wound up, and returned his abuse, there would have been two people needing PS treatment, and, who knows how many more people would have been caught up in the anger chain process!

There is another aspect to consider. If you can 'challenge yourself' to become a 'peacemaker' on a regular basis, and you can defuse rows and arguments whenever you encounter them, you will find that your gift has given you a 'buzz' of infinite satisfaction.

"Bless the road hogs?!"

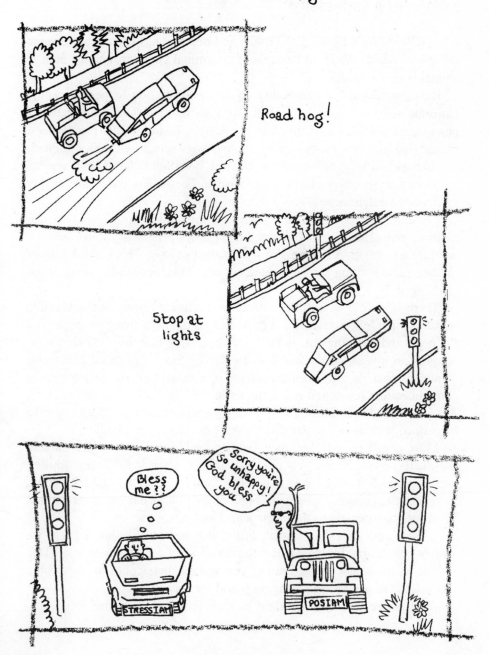

Part Two

TAMING OUR AGGRESSION

AGGRESSION IS AN INSTINCT and one that has been necessary for self-preservation. We see it throughout the animal kingdom, and the human animal is no exception.

But humankind has the ability to direct aggression to positive ends. Unfortunately, we lose control far too easily and our lurid national newspapers remind us of this fact regularly. To tackle this problem we should first look at some benign aggressive ways which we take for granted. For instance, a busy housewife tackles the household chores with vigour, vigorous activity being a form of aggression. Footballers and tennis players vigorously stretch themselves to win.

The human problem is that when we are under stress, emotion can highjack our aggressive instincts and change our personality so we become hateful and violent. A few pessimists amongst us say, "This is the nature of the beast and nothing can be done about it". This inevitability needs to be challenged.

There is an old saying that before you express anger, and aggressive stances which follow, one should gain composure by focusing on the area of the heart and counting ten. What I am suggesting that this idea should be adopted on a grand scale, and become the essence of civilised behaviour, something that has only been considered in a casual fashion. So saying, the communication revolution is helping us in this direction. Just before Hong Kong was handed to China, the opposing views of their leaders were able to be calmed with an eye to eye discussion... the 'counting ten effect'.

Most conflicts, whether they be personal, political or international, eventually burn themselves out but almost always following misery, hardship and suffering. It is imperative therefore that we embark upon a radical self-examination about our habit of unleashing our emotions without giving serious thought to the consequences of doing so.

What I am suggesting is that during this period of 'counting ten' we search our hearts for peaceful solutions and accept nothing less. This resolution is not just for the likes of you and me, but applies to responsible media and those who are managing world affairs.

Just as we teach our children to look left, look right and left again, before crossing the road, so the exploration of peaceful solutions to problems needs to become second nature.

Taming our aggression so it works for us in a positive manner, is positive and very possible. How about starting this trend tomorrow?

Note. For those interested in the concept of 'counting ten', which is another way of saying, 'time to reassess emotions', a process is going on. The awareness of an emotive issue is being re-located from the solar plexus area, (the source of our emotion), to the heart, (Higher-Self link).

For further guidance on this subject, refer to 'Help yourself to total freedom'. This can be obtained from 'Fringe Dwellers', address shown in index on closing pages.

KEEP YOUR COOL

THE CAR WON'T START. The kids are arguing and they are late for school. Tempers become frayed and you feel angry with life. You have become stressed, and have a headache to cap it!

The secret is to create a calming attitude to daily problems. This is not as difficult as it sounds and is quite easy if you put your mind to it.

Try becoming your own psychologist for a minute and approach the situation 'from outside looking in'. You will instantly get things in proportion and realise that relative to the real problems in the world, your problems are quite superficial.

What you also need when things seem to be getting out of hand is a pre-arranged plan to bring harmony and humour onto the scene. Here is one idea; every time problems build up, say in a loud voice, C.C.C. This stands for...we will be Cool, Calm, and Collect our thoughts positively.' If others copycat the idea, it creates some laughter which in itself is a 'happiness tonic'. This might sound naive, but try it. You will find that you can handle difficult situations with surprising calmness. What is more, it rubs off on all those around you. It works in the home, in the office, and even in the impatient queue at the supermarket.

It may not be your imagination that this self-therapy has made you a nicer person, along with the others around you. You see, it's catching!

Learning from Junior

Shouting and tears

young Tom butts in "C C C", both of you! Whats that, they ask?

C.C.C.

Teacher says we should all say C C C when we get cross! It means keep Cool, Calm and Collect happy thoughts!

CALLING ALL CELEBRITIES

IF YOU ARE A WELL KNOWN FIGURE IN PUBLIC LIFE, please take note.

The average person can only sow the seeds of caring and compassion in dribs and drabs, but not so with celebrities! They can sow ten thousand seeds in one go! You see, a high profile personality in the entertainment or sporting world can perform mini-miracles of immense value to the human race.

This may sound melodramatic, but their influence as role models on the hearts and souls of the younger generation, cannot be underestimated.

Bob Geldorf, Esther Rantzen, and Princess Diana, are typical examples of people in the public eye who have drawn attention to compassion by their charitable work.

Celebrities hold the eyes and ears of the populace, also their hearts, in contrast to teacher, parent, Priest or Rabbi, whose influence is more instructional and less inspiring.

Thus, in a magical way, young people can be tuned in to the kindlier side of human nature, and switch off from the negative hype to which we are all subjected.

Next time you sign an autograph, think whether your fame could be used to help the world in some positive way.

In your late years, when your fame has faded and your ego bruised, your spiritual achievement will give you an inner fulfilment. **You have done something to help the human race**.

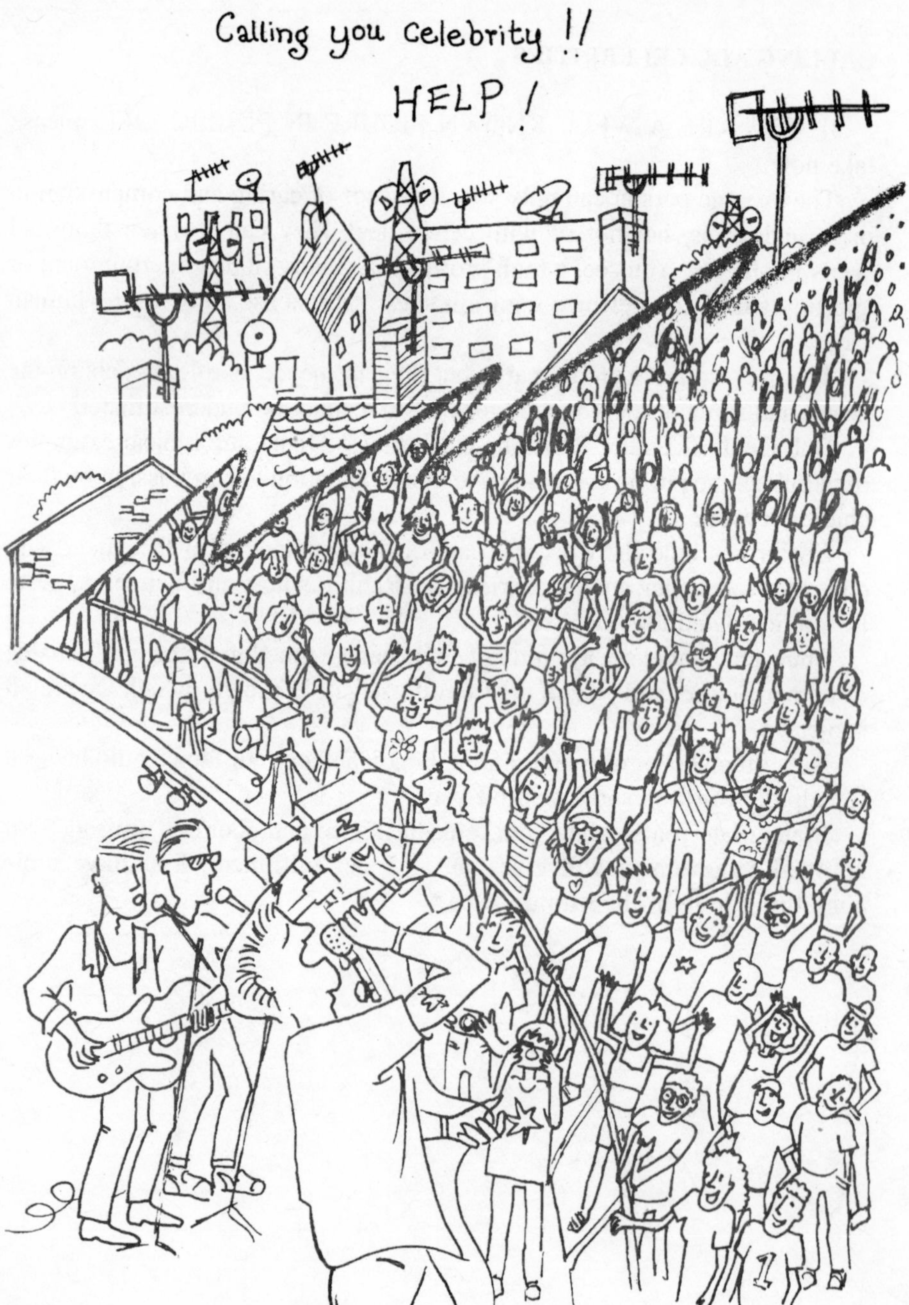
Calling you celebrity !!
HELP !

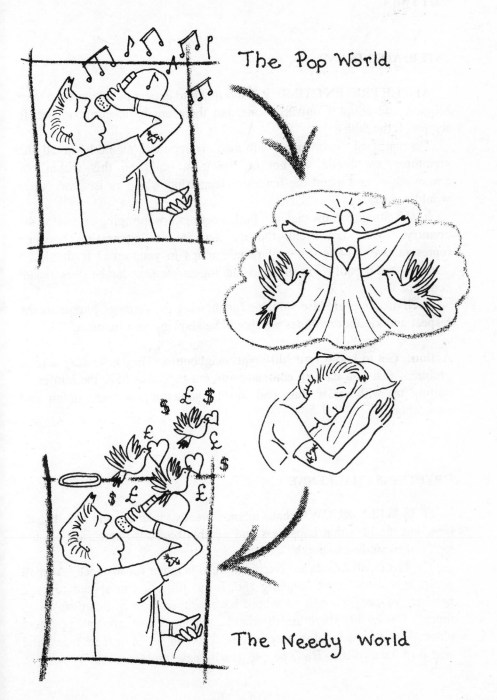

The Pop World

The Needy World

Part Two

INTERFAITH TREND

AT THE PRESENT TIME, it is too much to expect people to drop their religion and adopt a universal one, but there are basic common beliefs within all the faiths.

The spirit of 'goodwill to all men' is reported regularly in all the scriptures, so should we not be trying to build on this within our communities and mend the fences of friendship which racists and others would destroy?

It is exciting to know that interfaith meetings are springing up around the country. Why not break the ice and initiate a meeting between representatives of the different racial groups in your area? It should be informal and friendly, so real understanding and respect can be shown to all concerned.

Such meetings are also valuable for showing the younger generation the respect and kindlier attitudes we should be showing to minorities.

Action. Get to know your 'different' neighbours. They have very similar problems that you have to contend with, but they also have the burden of putting up with racist slurs and insults, something so very unfair and unacceptable.

GREETINGS CHALLENGE

IT IS WELL KNOWN that violence breeds violence, and hate breeds hate, but the idea that happiness and goodwill are also catching, has not really been studied in depth.

The fact is, all moods are catching. Take laughter for instance. A small group in a crowd start laughing and, in no time, it can spread to huge numbers of people, most of whom have neither seen or heard anything funny. Conversely there are thousands of people who are unhappy, feel unloved, and occasionally, very lonely. You can see it in their faces, and hear it in their voices. Rude people usually have problems too.

Most of us find it difficult to befriend such people, but there is one very simple method of setting the mood for happiness, and that is by being determined to greet people in a nice friendly sincere manner.

Just like courtesy shown to other car drivers, a trend can become a fashion, and a fashion can become a permanent behaviour pattern. The trend needs leaders to start the ball rolling. What about you and I?

Action. The more miserable people appear, the more cheering up they need! Challenge yourself to see how many people you can make smile or laugh each day. A gesture of friendship is reflected in a smile, and those who feel depressed or unhappy for some reason, need that uplift you give them. If it comes from your heart, your soul is developing and you will feel happiness growing within yourself as well!

BREAKING THE CRIME CYCLE

WE KNOW that much crime originates from youngsters going astray for a number of reasons. Most of these are due to lack of positive outlets for their energy but also they are contaminated by selfishness and violence, expressed in newspapers, TV, videos etc.

But just imagine if you lived in a rundown neighbourhood where your children were constantly exposed to drug addiction, shoplifting and joy riding. It would be an uphill struggle to portray caring and worthy values with so much 'competition'.

Crime therefore has to be tackled at source and not by just shutting criminals away.

It is a degrading element of successive governments that they pander to the lowest instinct of revenge, a basic negative emotion. They repeat what an emotive public like to hear, 'criminals must be punished more severely. We should build more prisons'

In ancient time, rabble rousers used to shout 'off with their heads' and were encouraged by rulers who needed distraction from their own shortcomings.

Shutting criminals away in a 'crime' factory, is as soul destroying as it is nonsensical! At the end of their term of imprisonment, criminals will have been trained to become more efficient at their 'craft'.

Those who arrive in prison, should be taught skills and perform community tasks, helping victims and those in distress.

Reports have shown that many criminals who become closely involved in helping those in need, and even the victims of crime, become motivated to lead good honest lives. Victims of crime should seriously dwell on these points as the final issue must be to reduce the number of victims.

But for the grace of God, you or I could be that person who went astray in childhood!

Action. Join prison reform organisations to put pressure on the government to change the present negative attitude towards the rehabilitation of prisoners and prevention of crime.

'I COULD BE YOU'

TURN OFF your usual train of thought and fantasise for a moment.

Suppose the Almighty had decided you should have entered the world in the form of a fish, a giraffe or a bird!

A more down-to-earth thought would be to consider each person you meet in a new positive light, namely, 'that person in front of me could have been me, if God had chosen it so!

This kind of thought need not be a fantasy if you think it through a bit. Indeed, there are some profound implications which will tell you that you can be a 'healer'. A healer of friction, misunderstanding and even hate. This needs clarifying.

Almost every problem in the home, in the office, in society, and on the world scene, centres round not being able to see the other person's point of view. How much easier it is to do so, if you have trained yourself to automatically do that very thing.

There is a knock-on effect too, because an 'I could be you' theme can

80

become a 'virus' from which there is no cure. An exciting concept for universal goodwill which you are helping to introduce.

Action. Challenge yourself to adopt the idea of terminating even minor conflicts in a positive way as described above. After a time, there will be no effort involved, because it will have become a natural healing feature of your character.

YOU CAN CHANGE THE WORLD!

Are you a young person unable to land a job, feel depressed and bored with low self-esteem? Well, I have news for you! Every person has a part to play, in some form or other, to do something positive for the world.

You are needed, so cheer up and think positively about your capabilities. If you have the will, you can do wonders!

The turn-off at the job centre is not the end of the world and perhaps can be the beginning!

Note. There is an organisation called National Youth Agency which provides numerous alternative possibilities for helping people and communities. For teachers and youth workers, they offer a directory of global youth work resources entitled 'Changing the World' (address in closing pages).

LAUGHING TONIC

WHEN OUR SPIRITS ARE LOW, there is nothing like laughter to obtain a sense of well-being. It is a fact that the fun of childhood always lies in our subconscious mind and it should be brought to the surface at regular intervals to brighten our lives and those around us.

Medical opinion points to laughter having actual healing powers for both mind and body.

It is literally a health tonic, for it stimulates circulation and parts of the body which enhance body immunity.

We may yet live to see laughing exercises available on the NHS, something which may save large numbers of pills and queues at the doctors' surgeries.

God has given us a sense of humour so let us use it to brighten up our lives and especially those who desperately need someone to talk to, such as pensioners, the depressed and those who are caught up in worries and family problems.

Goodwill and humour are closely related, and if you can build humour into friendly conversation, it will be like icing on the 'cake of happiness'. There is a saying which sums up the situation,

'Laugh and the whole world laughs with you,

Cry and you cry alone because compassion, just at present, is in short supply'.

Action. When someone looks miserable, let that be the 'switch on' for a challenge in your mind. The challenge is, make that person happy and if laughter can raise his or her spirits, you have done your deed for the day

Laughter on the NHS

where did we go
wrong Samantha?

where did we go
wrong Suzy?

ONE GOD-HEAD

POSITIVE SPIRIT ENCOURAGES the concept of one God, intent on bringing us all into a spiritual union of Godliness. But this requires each person to appreciate the other's religious interpretation of God, in a spirit of brotherhood, something which has to be encouraged.

Few people realise how similar are the main basic values and ethics amongst the various religions of the world. Extracts from their holy scriptures are listed below to illustrate this fact.

From these, one can see that the basis of all the main religions of the world, include an element of caring for others.

There are Jews alongside Christians manning the Samaritans.

Pramod is a Hindu in Bradford, and is one from a group of volunteers who visit ill old people in hospital. His Guru says, 'love mankind and serve all'.

If your religion inspires you to bring out the Positive Spirit within you, and you can love the ones who find a different route, you are joining others in the quest for love and harmony in the human race.

Even those who never frequent holy places, can be spiritually alive. The philosophy of Positive Spirit unearths the loving attributes in the souls of most unlikely people. Religious and ethnic bigotry have no place in this forward looking philosophy.

Brahmanism: "This is the sum of duty. Do naught unto others which would cause pain unto you"...Mahabharate 5, 1517.

Buddhism: "Hurt not others in ways that you yourself would find hurtful"...Udana-Varga 5,18.

Christianity: "All things whatsoever ye should wish that men should do to you, do you even so to them"... Matthew, 7, 12.

Judaism: "What is hateful to you, do not do to your fellow men"...Talmud, Shabbat. 31a.

Confucianism: "It is loving kindness that you do not do unto others that you would not have them do to you"...Analects 15,23.

Islam: "No one is a believer until he desires for his brother that which he desires for himself"...Sunni.

Taoism: "Regard your neighbour's gain as your own gain and your neighbour's loss as your own loss"...T'ai Shang Kan Ying P'ien.

Action. If you have a religious leaning, enquire at your Church, Synagogue, Mosque, or other place of worship as to how you can help the world in some small way. It needs you!

But if you have a leaning just for caring, compassion, and positive activities outside of religion, do not feel unqualified.

Your soul and loving goodwill will give you more fulfilment than those who preach these things but often forget to practice them !

INFANTS OF TODAY-SHAPERS OF TOMORROW

HERE ARE SOME THOUGHTS for parents or guardians.

Did you know that from infancy your child is picking up every emotion, strong word, argument, and feeling which it encounters in your home? It cannot tell you this, but deep inside, all these things register in it's unconscious mind, and these will be reflected in the future character, moods, and behaviour of the child as it grows up.

Children need a full complement of love within a framework of fair discipline. If they are shown affection, fairness, and real friendship, these attributes will be planted in their souls for ever, and they will pass them on to their children. Conversely if they are ill-treated, feel unloved, insecure, or live in a violent atmosphere, they may perpetuate the same into generations

Infants of today
Shapers of tomorrow

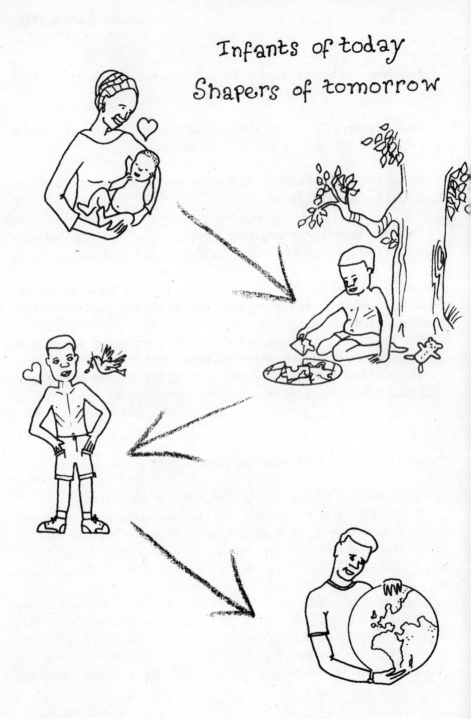

to come.

Multiply one child by a billion, and one can see how the future harmony of the world relates to the environment we create for the young generation.

Action. To parents who feel unable to cope with their children's welfare, do not feel downhearted, but apply for help from addresses supplied. You owe it to yourself and your kids to do so !

Those whose circumstances have enabled them to give their children the support they need, should in turn support agencies pledged to assist families with problems in these matters. Helpful addresses are shown in the index.

DAILY SOUL CHALLENGE

DID YOU KNOW that we all have the power to perform mini-miracles to help humanity in a thousand little ways?

We need not be religious in the normal accepted sense, but one thing is needed before anything else. We must have a sincere feeling in our hearts that we would love, in some way or other, to improve the world and make it a happier place to live in.

If you are a candidate, you should first 'challenge your soul' to give you the power to make every person you meet who looks sad or troubled, happier and content with life. After a while, you will find that your soul becomes attuned naturally to the process. You will have become both a nicer person and a happier one. Curiously, the people you meet will become imbued with benevolence. It will not be just your imagination!

The explanation is that God has provided us with the means of drawing on spiritual power in order to perform such mini-miracles. It is the spiritual evolution process of making humans kindlier and less aggressive. It is a slow process, but we can hurry it along each in our own little way!

Such ideas are often sneered at by sceptics who are insensitive to higher things. Usually such people have been short of love in their early lives, and their souls are bruised and resentful.

More and more people are finding that 'healing' thoughts in some miraculous way, do actually work. It is the basis of many religions.

Try it out and be convinced. Thousands have already been, and millions will be, as 'outgoing' soul power will surely be recognised, not as paranormal, but very normal.

ENERGY TO SPARE?

HAVE YOU GOT ENERGY to spare and a will to do something positive for humanity?

You do not need to be a fitness fanatic. There are disabled people getting a buzz from actively helping others with disabilities.

It is all a question of how we value our responsibilities for having been given a mind and body with 'spare capacity' and doing some good with it!

How about taking a 'human help holiday' which might involve helping disaster victims following the aftermath of war or an earthquake? One group in a coach went to Sarajevo to rebuild an infants' school razed to the ground during hostilities, but the quest could be refurbishing a building for the homeless in your own neighbourhood.

God has blessed many of us with an active mind and body together with a soul, but this needs 'nudging' occasionally to get it going!

If you think about it, any one of us could one day be in desperate need for a helping hand.

Positive Spirit building

Ego strength

P.S. strength

Part Two

'PLUG INTO GOODWILL' AND RADIATE

HAVE YOU FOUND A WAY of temporarily 'leaving' this hectic world and finding peace of mind, perhaps in your garden or in the unspoilt countryside?

Perhaps you practice meditation or other forms of relaxation. But providing you can 'turn off' from daily routine problems and put your thoughts onto a higher plane, you can be a 'goodwill creator' and a 'healer' of sorts. This needs explaining.

Creating goodwill involves 'kick-starting' one's soul from the moment of awakening. For instance, upon rising, make a simple resolution, 'all thoughts and deeds today will be helpful and considerate' This involves thinking positively about every situation you encounter just as though it was a challenge for you to do so. It will be strange at first, unless your nature is already of a generous nature. But persevere for several weeks and don't give up. In due course your soul will 'go creative' naturally.

After a while, the things that normally annoy you about people, will cease to do so, as you will find yourself 'entering their shoes' and knowing why they do what they do.

All this does not mean you have become religious with saintly powers in the conventional sense so dispel any ideas of grandeur. Anyone can tune into the spiritual wave length channel if their thoughts are full of goodwill and kindness.

But, what is exciting is that almost without trying, one can spread this soul-enhancing process. There can be few things more fulfilling!

UNEMPLOYMENT, NO STIGMA!

WE HAVE ALREADY reached the age when machines are designed to do jobs quicker and better than humans.

As the Far East industrialises, and products from that area are released into the Western world, competition will be stepped up, and jobs will be in short supply. But this need not be a doomsday scenario. On the contrary, it is a shift of emphasis of the human spirit. Do we degenerate when we may need to give up some of our luxuries. Were we really happy when we had them all?

Clearly, people will have even more time on their hands than they do now, and a plan of intent should be visualised now, not later!

Unemployment is not a shameful state of existence, unless you are doing nothing positive with your spare time.

True, it is harder to budget on dole money or part-time work, but we in the West have become to accept that a house should have numerous electrical gadgets, often two cars per family, and a host of luxuries, which fifty years ago would have been unthinkable. We must therefore accept that a different standard of living is inevitable. Different, because new positive fulfilments will arise, creating a new standard of motivation for living.

Unpaid employment may not sound attractive, but there are hundreds of occupations which pay little or nothing from a monetary point of view but are very rewarding and fulfilling.

There is no excuse to feel bored or useless, as numerous charities need our particular skills and energy.

Thousands will vouch how voluntary work can give one a buzz. It's a feeling of comradeship with others to make the world a nicer place to live in.

Note. There are now lists of charities, in which you can become involved, part time or full time. You can be solving problems in your local community or further afield, even in a third world country!

No time like the present to make enquiries!

ENJOY YOUR FOOD?

YOU HAVE JUST ENJOYED a nice four-course meal, when a scene on the television shows African children barely alive, just skin and bones? Do you feel uncomfortable?

Would you happily have gone without your meal, if only that pathetic scene could be redressed by doing so?

If so, you have a spiritual potential of unselfishness, ready for development. It is your soul 'speaking' as it were.

There are numerous charities devoted to alleviating hunger and suffering in third world countries. Some charities which assist farm communities to help themselves are the most effective. Receiving purely 'gift charity' can be demoralising.

Alternatively, your local community may need you. Often, there are hungry, homeless and desperate people 'on your doorstep'

Action. Should you be unemployed, retired, or been made redundant, don't mope and feel a personal lack of self esteem. There are many ways of being fulfilled. It may not be rewarding financially, but helping others gives one a good feeling inside. You are needed!

Two faces of hunger

Part Two

HOW TO LOVE YOURSELF!

SELF-LOVE sounds like a recipe for conceit and pride, but the brand referred to here, is not the "I'm better than you" variety. It is an expression of "soul love".

To explain this further. When one feels an urge to do a good deed, the soul is in control of the personality.

After helping a blind person across the road or cheering up an ill acquaintance, there has been no apparent benefit to yourself. You would be wrong though! What you have done is to create a 'self love situation' You feel good and you feel loved inside, yet you are both the giver and the receiver!

It may be difficult to understand but the love and compassion you have shown has bounced back into your soul. You are loving yourself without realising it, and being loved is great even if you are the perpetrator!

Footnote. We are often totally occupied with our own problems and worries, and would welcome someone to share them with. Helping other people in some strange way, enables one to bear one's own burdens in a more tranquil manner.

In brief, if we impart love, compassion, and goodwill, we not only spread these wonderful things but we receive them back in the form of 'loving contentment'.

TIME CLOCK FOR PEACE

Peace Clock

THOUSANDS OF PEOPLE at a fixed time, 12 A.M. in the country they reside, pray for peace for a full minute. Peace between races! Peace between countries! Peace in the home!

This is called the TIME CLOCK for PEACE.

If you would like to join Prayers for Peace, first relax and clear your mind of problems and imagine a world of tranquillity and beauty. Then imagine that you are a contributor to this harmony. Then you are ready to convey healing thoughts in the form of a prayer for peace.

Positive thoughts on the 'soul wave band' can work wonders especially when joined in unison with thousands of others.

Pray through your religion if you feel inspired to do so. But the point is, you must be confident your prayers will get through. If you have faith, they will do so!

When peace comes to a conflict, it could be one close at hand or in a distant land, but never doubt that you have made a small but vital contribution to attaining it.

Here is one prayer, but you can make up your own as you wish,

> Please let my peaceful thoughts join others.
> To spread love from one person to another.
> To give compassion to all beings in need of it.
> To send joy and serenity to all beings.

You are helping the world in your own small way. God will not send you a letter of thanks but your heart will tell you that your message is getting through!

Part Two

OPTIMISM WINS THROUGH

DOES YOUR DAILY NEWSPAPER upset you with it's negative news, describing violence and crime so regularly and vividly? Well, I have news for you. Britain, as a whole, is one of the most safest places to live in the world. When a horrible crime is committed, say in London, it reaches the headlines, and puts fear into it's residents, but the population of London is twelve million, this being more than the population of Australia and New Zealand put together. London also has more inhabitants than Holland, Austria or Belgium, and double that of most Scandinavian countries.

It is therefore important to get everything in life in proportion, and realise that our minds and thoughts can shape the future in a positive manner if we approach the problems we encounter both calmly and optimistically.

In a span of 50 years, the world has been transformed and not all in a bad way. It will surprise many to know that aspirations for human rights, charitable activities and peaceful gestures are now on an upward trend. More and more young people are opting to work and support good causes in third world countries.

But even if the world was going down hill, it was man who let it slide that way and what an exciting challenge this presents!

The following should be reproduced in bold lettering alongside the utterances of our doom predictors:-

Optimism breeds hope... Hope breeds challenge
Challenge breeds motivation.
Motivation is the cradle of achievement.

BULLYING AT SCHOOL

WHERE DOES THE BULLY come from? In childhood, he or she has often been at the receiving end of harassment, humiliation, abuse or violence, probably within the family unit.

It is a sad fact that those who receive such treatment in their very early years, often impart the same treatment on others in the playground.

A survey of young bullies also shows that they usually show violent criminal tendencies in adolescence. A bully today, a mugger tomorrow?

Action. If you suspect your child is being bullied at school, report it to the head teacher at once, before the injustice festers. Schools now have special procedures to eradicate bullying.

But when you have children, remember your responsibility to the next generation, and if you feel your child is becoming a bully, seek help. Were you abused in some way yourself and you feel the urge to abuse? If so, seek help without delay. There is nothing to be ashamed of, but you must do it!

Bringing up children in some circumstances can be fraught with problems. Be happy to know there is help is on hand. Refer to addresses in index.

violence breeds violence

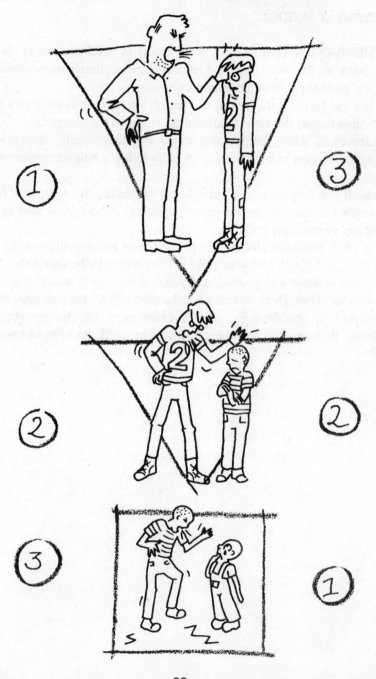

UNDER-ACHIEVER?

BY WHAT RIGHT do we judge a young person to be a failure?

There are a score of reasons why your child has not performed well at school. He or she may be dyslectic, or just a slow developer.

More often than not, the school is at fault in not spotting a lateral thinker with a creative mind

There can be hidden talents lying unrecognised within hobbies or artistic trends.

It is a fact that creative young people rarely excel in history, but they are infinitely better at visualising the mistakes which history exposes.

A child who was a 'dreamer' and considered somewhat 'thick' became a world famous writer of children's books. She gave joy to thousands of children, a feat which so called 'clever ones' would find it hard to match!

Remember, everyone is good at something!

Note. Never undermine the confidence of your children or underestimate their potential. Even if reports from school are disappointing, if they are doing their best, praise them for trying. This will uplift their self-esteem which is vital for a well-balanced personality.

Under- achiever ?

CHARLOTTE

1995 AD
Charlotte, age 10
sitting at desk -
dreaming of animals

Animals of the world

By charlotte Smith

Best seller!
Famous Charlotte
2010 AD

MEDITATE AND CONTEMPLATE

THE PHILOSOPHY OF POSITIVE SPIRIT can be introduced people by a number of routes. One gentle way is to take up meditation, something which is becoming increasingly popular amongst those who feel the need to 'turn off' from the stressful life we, in the West, have imposed on ourselves.

Yoga is especially helpful to the PS cause, because in addition to physical exercises to improve health and posture, it points to positive attitudes in living and thinking.

The meditation in Yoga encourages peaceful thoughts and spiritual well-being. Those who practice it and study all facets of the subject will find a close resemblance to ideas expressed within the Positive Spirit philosophy.

Yoga emphasises the need to seek harmony of the spirit, with peace and goodwill being essential ingredients to attain it. It is, therefore, a valuable stepping stone to Positive Spirit enlightenment.

Note. Almost every medium-sized town has social activities and classes in a range of subjects which include Yoga and meditation. If in doubt, refer to the British School of Yoga who will advise you (address in index).

Part Two

'THERE'S A FLY IN MY SOUP'

When we are stressed or under pressure, it is sometimes difficult to keep one's cool. One can become irrational and even aggressive. The most important thing is to find a means of getting things in perspective, and reducing the 'mountains', which 99% of the time are really 'mole hills'.

This story may bring this home to you.

A stressed man in a restaurant (Mr X) is served soup, in which he has observed a fly floating on top. To the waiter, he shouts 'What sort of dump is this? Get the manager. It's disgusting!"

The waiter feels miserable. The manager shouts at his staff to be more careful. The other diners are embarrassed.

However, from an adjoining table, a man comes up to Mr X, and says, "I'm from Oxfam, and I've just come back from Somalia. Children would be scrambling over themselves just to lick your plate of soup. Your fly would be the cherry on the cake. You should be ashamed of yourself."

A shameful silence fell on the scene. All those in the restaurant contemplated the contrast between the behaviour of the 'haves' and the fate of the 'have nots'.

Action. Whenever you find yourself 'blowing your top' over something relatively trivial, you can train your soul to get things into perspective. The above story will help to do this. Just think of the word 'soup' and this will be the magic subconscious word which will prevent a tiff, argument, or row. People will wonder how you have become a more reasonable person. If you tell them it is 'soup', you will get a funny look, but no matter, it will stick in their mind. You will have perhaps have sown a healing seed in their soul too!

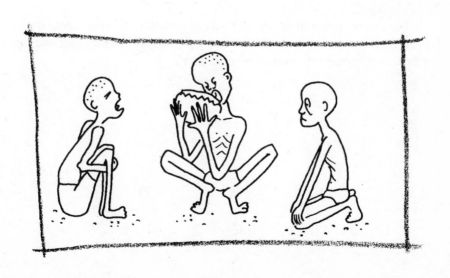

Part Two

COMPASSION IS STRONG

THERE ARE SOME amongst us who mistakenly believe that unreserved compassion is weak, but how wrong they are. We all have seeds of kindness and compassion within us and we should be proud of it. Here is a true example to support this view.

British commandos, tough as they come and trained to kill rather than save, were sent on a rescue mission to Iraq. On arrival at their destination, some of them literally shed tears at the plight of the Kurd families driven from their homes and now stranded up in the bleak snow covered mountains.

The quest for rescuing innocents caught up in other people's wars, was admirable in itself, but the personal feelings of compassion displayed by the rescuers as they bundled them into their helicopters, was something rather special. No matter that they were of different faith, race and culture. They were fellow human beings in misery!

The rescued must have thought..."these people coming from the skies to help us...how wonderful! But what do they get out of it, they are not one of us?"

The rescuers on the other hand, were thinking.... "my God, these poor b.......... caught up in this wretched place. We've got to get them out of this hell-hole fast!"

What can we learn from this true story? It is this. Without compassion, humankind is sterile and if we display it with enthusiasm we are harmonising human relations as never before!

ONE RACE, THE HUMAN RACE!

THERE IS A HUMAN FAILING which comes to the surface when things become tough. It can be unemployment, money problems, or family breakdown. This creates frustration and some of us search for a scapegoat to release our tension on someone else. That is when our sense of fairness and compassion temporarily goes out of the window, for so often minorities of different faith, race, or religion, become the target of pent-up anger.

In a 'scapegoat search' mentality, one can become a different person, a racist and a bully, devoid of compassion.

Like minds join forces and in no time, you have a group of people intent on harassing people to blame for their misfortunes. It happened to a whole nation, Nazi Germany.

Don't let this happen to you or your children!

Action. It would be so helpful to impress on our children at an early age, that, 'but for the grace of God', we could be a minority living rather insecurely amongst others who profess to be fair minded but so often do not live up to being so.

Even at play school, we can "sow the seed" to the toddlers, and express the lovely variety of people there are in the world, and like the range of flowers and plants, we should love them and protect them.

Who am I ?

Joe Matts speaks at National Front meeting

" Send all the blacks home "

Back- at home in Brixton, his mother says

" I have something important to tell you "

" I am not your real mother. We adopted you as a baby.

Your mother came from Jamaica and . . -

SHY 'DO-GOODERS'

THE MEDIA CLAIM to provide what the people like in the form of sensational and dramatic news. In the process, truth is distorted and characters are smeared by innuendo, and exaggerations.

At times, leading figures in our society are brought down to earth with a scandal. This has resulted in it becoming fashionable to sneer at all those who are genuinely doing good deeds as though they are by nature insincere and looking for praise.

The media who are often searching for a 'bad apple', will crucify anyone who has even a small 'skeleton in the cupboard', so it is small wonder that many thousands of good-hearted people are inclined to hesitate before aligning themselves with good causes. The fear of being ridiculed and negatively labelled, worries their families.

But do not be put of off. People who try to humiliate those who show goodwill and a caring nature are really ill in their hearts. Psychologists will confirm that such people have been hurt in their earlier lives, and are vengeful, and resentful.

'Do-gooders' therefore unite and dismiss those who like to humiliate you. They are to be pitied, and cannot be happy people.

Part Two

ALL THE SAME 'UNDERNEATH'

FIRST DWELL on the fact that children have no inborn racial or colour prejudice, but they do notice differences.

Children's minds are like magnets, and since naughtiness is part of the growing up process, they quickly pick up any negative traits from their elders. Their souls therefore need bolstering should they encounter racial prejudice.

So from the earliest age, impress on young children the wonderful variety of humans in the world, along with the colourful flowers and birds with whom we share the earth.

By imaginative portrayal of what life is like in another country, they will learn to feel what it is like to 'be in someone else's shoes', should God have decided that their mummy or daddy had been born there.

Ask children to imagine how strange our white skin and round eyes must appear to people living in Mongolia.

By instilling positive attitudes towards the human family at an early age, they will instinctively accept and respect those 'different' people amongst us. A real PS soul development exercise!

HATE OUT, LOVE IN

ONE RELIGION SUGGESTS we should love our enemies. This is difficult to swallow. But since by the grace of God you might have been born the child of your enemies' parents, hating someone personally is nonsense. This should not be confused with hating their actions.

From childhood, we must learn therefore not to react emotionally when confronted with rude or hateful people, but seek the causes of their behaviour.

Hate breeds hate, so being nice to that grumpy person will take him or her off her guard, and show the nonsense of confrontation.

So very often, managers who wield power, become aggressive to their underlings, and the stress even filters down to the telephone operator, her voice reflecting the mood of the people who work in the company.

People who are unpleasant are usually people who are unhappy. If you can instill this realisation into your subconscious mind, you will be able to defuse confrontations and be more reasonable yourself. It is encouraging to know that a friendly atmosphere catches on fast.

The philosophy of Positive Spirit encourages this kindlier aspect of human nature. It is a positive trend which can spread quickly into every sphere of life.

A trend of 'love to replace hate' is within the capacity of all humans and isn't it so much more agreeable too?

Part Two

CHILDLINE IS YOUR LINE

AT LEAST TEN THOUSAND cries for help are received daily by the charity, Childline. Their cries refer to their pitiful suffering from abuse, physical, sexual and mental. For every voice heard there are at least five silent ones, those being the ones too frightened to reach for the telephone.

Terrible things are said and done to children by parents and others, often without thought to the consequences.

It is a fact that abused children, become abusers themselves and so we should try and catch them before they are permanently damaged. But in the longer term, we must find means of breaking the 'abuse chain' before it becomes an epidemic.

Violence in all it's forms perpetuates a copycat process, but this can be reversed if we all take a positive role in tackling the problem at a very early age. Children who are withdrawn or disruptive in class need special treatment because these are the tell-tale signs of instability and anti-social behaviour in later life.

Action. Join organisations to tackle the root causes of child cruelty in all it's forms.

If you are a parent and inclined to take it out on your children, or perhaps suspect your child is being molested, call the authorities. Counsellors from Parent Help Line understand these problems and gladly offer you help, (address in index)

EMPLOYERS, PLEASE NOTE.

DOES YOUR FIRM employ twenty-five people or more? If so, how about adopting a village or community in a Third World country?

Your employees, like most people, are rarely able to get involved in charitable causes on their own. By sponsoring projects in the third world, and involving both management and staff in the process, you are boosting that caring instinct that most people have, but rarely find time to express it.

The philosophy of Positive Spirit is involved in bridging the gaps which divide humans across the world. This is one of many ideas to attain that 'caring' concept, which the world needs so desperately.

The Third World needs helping hands to enable them to help them themselves, and not just hand-outs. Remember they are our neighbours, only a second away by satellite and a few hours by plane.

But for the grace of God, you or I could be that person struggling to live in a harsh climate without running water and barely enough food to feed one's children let alone oneself!

Wanted... neighbours who care!

Smithsons Co. Ltd - England

Maroda Community - Sudan

VALUE GOOD NATURE

A MYTH NEEDS exposing as soon as possible. For an eternity we have been brain-washed into believing that human nature is basically evil and that our aim in life is to keep it in check by injecting "goodness"

Throughout history we see a trend to purge out the perceived sin in us. The Spanish inquisition were experts and committed unpardonable sins themselves in the process.

The sooner this notion is turned on its head, the sooner can love and goodwill be released from a prison of guilt. No longer will there be that hindrance of "being found guilty of a crime before it has been committed"

Becoming unkind, greedy, savage or just unpleasant, is not an inherited human nature, they are traits we learn from parents or peers.

The assumption that human nature has a strong evil content is therefore badly flawed. It mistakes the effect for the cause.

We should therefore rejoice in our caring and loving instincts and enthuse in the knowledge that we can squeeze out the evils we encounter by revelling in our good nature.

Let us feel good about our human nature and spread those feelings around. Watch out evil, you are on the way out!

Feeling good with your nature

Our loving nature

Guilt hidden nature

BEEN MADE REDUNDANT?

THE WORD 'REDUNDANT' suggests one is no longer of any use, which is absolute nonsense. In times to come, there may be a vast labour force with little full-time commercial employment in sight.

Are we all going to jump off a cliff ?

Whilst earning a good living may seem the most important thing in your life, one can obtain fulfilment of a different kind.

Our skills, whatever they may be, are desperately needed by charities and community activities.

Don't doubt it, we are urgently needed by people who are struggling with too few volunteers.

You may be a redundant aircraft fitter. Could you connect a Land Rover power drive to a water pump in Bangladesh? You might be the only one who could!

Are you a redundant BT engineer? What a Godsend you would be in Somalia, where you could teach the locals how to repair their broken communication system!

Unlike the Job Centre, there are vastly more jobs than people to fill them. Here are a few samples of activities, where we are needed.

Helping youngsters in inner cities.　Farm implements for Ethiopia.
Housing the homeless.　Workshop for the disabled.
Blankets for earthquake victims.　Help line for children.
Toys for deprived children.　Printing of charity leaflets.
Outings for the handicapped.　Running a boy's club.
Managing an inner city's football team.

Fulfilment

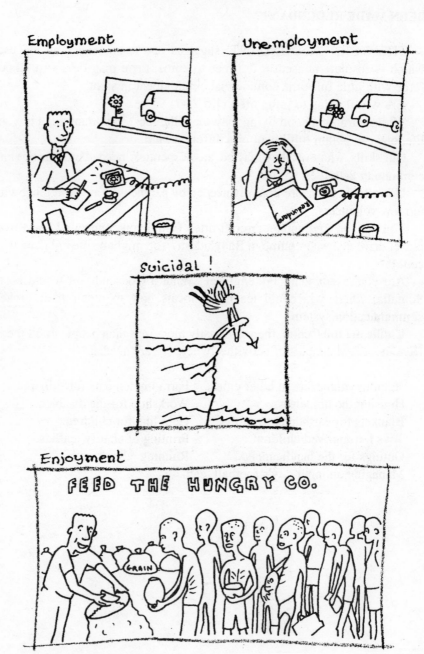

POSITIVE AWAKENING THOUGHTS

IF YOU HAVE already practised "Positive bedtime thinking" you will awaken in the morning with a feeling of mild elation, which says, 'there's a purpose in my life....lets live it!"

But to express this positive statement which tells you that your soul is "active for service", you will want to put to put it into operation.

So speak to your soul, and decide, "this week I shall do at least two good deeds to help my family or my community or the world at large"

Then decide, "I will handle any stressful problems today, calmly and in a happy frame of mind together with the utmost concern for others involved".

PART THREE

RELIGIOUS AND SPIRITUAL ASPECTS

BRIDGING THE GOD GAP

THE WAY THE MEDIA draws attention to religious conflicts around the world, one would think that the worlds' faiths were opposites, whereas in fact they mostly aspire to similar basic laws on moral behaviour.

The phrase, 'Only do to others, as you would be done by', occurs right across the scriptures, phrased differently in six world religions. Over thousands of years, it was living conditions, climate and geography, which caused people to interpret their God in diverse ways. The human soul and it's potential for harmony crosses every barrier of geography and race.

But the problem remains that there is a stalemate of genuine 'brotherly feeling' between people of various faiths, because religious differences have become entrenched in the political framework of the countries.

If truth will have it, most of us have been indoctrinated that our God will frown on our expressing any affection for other versions of God worship.

But we are now in a so-called enlightened age, and spiritual bridges are desperately needed. The idea of strictly observing different 'instructions' for the same 'mind body', defies logic.

Even in a multi-cultural society, the idea of creating a hybrid 'religion for all', immediately polarises the various faiths for several reasons. Culture is closely bound up with religion, and the very idea of a 'Godhead' is felt to depreciate the value of faith and culture simultaneously.

In industry today, one could be working alongside a friendly good-natured colleague with a dark complexion, who wears a turban. He shares the same joy, pain, and problems as his white counterpart and who is to say whether his version of Godliness is inferior or superior to another? Is it not what a person says and does in his or her lifetime, which requires judging?

One source of the problem is the question of multi-faith schooling which is in disarray, because the concept is questioned with some passion by religious leaders who see their faith being 'contaminated'. They see multi-faith teaching as a 'mish-mash' with nothing solid to promote spiritual and moral development. I believe that the Positive Spirit philosophy can fill that supposed vacuum, as it is overflowing with the most inspiring notions of goodwill, peace, respect and generosity.

I am optimistic for other reasons. There are already a 'meeting of minds' at the United Nations, and this may well be a a stepping stone for a 'meeting of faiths', leading eventually to a 'meeting of hearts. Perhaps a 'Spiritual Commonwealth of Nations" could become an appendage of the United Nations, so the word 'united' would become meaningful and realistic.

With cheaper air travel on the horizon and work permits becoming more international, the presence of "different" people amongst us will become commonplace. Fifty years from now, inter-marriage and social contact in the workplace will complete the picture of a relaxed multiracial society

But in the meantime, there are other bases upon which religious harmony can be built. One is the Interfaith Network, which now has affiliations across the world. Another promising development is the British Meditation Society's "symbol of light" which encourages an essential unity of all the faiths.

When an Arab can hug a Jew, or when a Hindu can hug a Moslem and not feel they are betraying their faiths, then we are on the road to humankind's spiritual salvation. Are not all religions in Israel founded on a shared prophet, Abraham? As I write this statement, it has been announced that Arafat and Rabin, two of the most 'extremes' in the Middle East, are to shake hands in a gesture of peaceful coexistence. This proves that anything is possible if the will is there for peace and harmony!

Here are extracts from declarations given by religious leaders on the occasion of an Interfaith meeting at Assisi in Italy (1986). The occasion was the 25th anniversary of the WWF. It is significant that the theme of harmony and goodwill extends to all creatures, including the human animal. Religions are listed in alphabetical order:-

BUDDHISM

'Our religion is based on love, understanding and compassion. It is committed to respect and happiness for all sentient beings. We believe all disputes should be settled in a non-violent way.

As co-inhabitants of this earth, the other beings have the same right of protection as humans enjoy. They should not be exploited by humans.'

CHRISTIANITY

'Christians call upon all men and women to pursue truth, justice, and peaceful coexistence with all peoples, so love and compassion can universally prevail. Furthermore it is God's will and design, in the name of Christ, that all forms of activity which encourage wars, discriminations and destruction of cultures, should be repudiated.'

HINDUISM

'With the example of Mahatma Ghandi, we have a special reverence for all life on earth, which includes humans, animals, and plant life. We oppose violence in all it's forms.'

The divine purpose of God is to encourage the beauty and harmony in this world, which is in danger from the unrestrained zest for technical achievement.'

ISLAM

'Islam has the dual meaning of submission to God and the peace it creates, that is peace within us, peace between man and man, also between man and nature.

Unity of mankind cannot be achieved with discord, only with harmony.

The world is green and beautiful and God has appointed us his guardians. We should adopt such values in all our relationships and wisdoms.'

JUDAISM

'The Talmud states that heaven rewards the person who has concern and compassion for all humanity and the rest of creation.

We have a responsibility to God for creating the utmost harmony, for we are all passengers in the same fragile floating world. Let us safeguard our rowing boat by all of us rowing together in unison.'

SIKHISM

'We Sikhs proclaim the glory of God in nature and the environment.

All creatures are blessed and humans living on this earth must be seen to keep to righteous activities.

God, as both Father and Mother, guarantees equality to man and women in faith and compassion towards all beings'

Conclusion. Declarations made at Assisi by representatives of the world's main religions were most encouraging. It pointed to the fact that there is a universal human desire for peace and tranquillity between the tribes of the planet, and that eventually harmony must prevail.

It also confirmed that the human race were in one accord about the responsibilities we share for looking after the environment and caring for animals and all forms of life on the planet.

DOES GOD HEAR US?

THE TIMES NEWSPAPER raised an interesting question following calls for prayers on behalf of Terry Waite, whose kidnapping by terrorists in Lebanon, caused such universal anguish in the Christian world. The question was raised by some sceptics as to whether prayers sent by thousands of people for his well-being, were really helpful in obtaining his release and restoring his full health

Most scientists refuse to accept that thoughts and healing can travel through space, but if such people claim to be religious, there is a contradiction of loyalties.

Theologians, and other spiritual believers, on the other hand, are adamant that prayer works, providing the sender has conviction and faith.

But such happenings are now opening scientific minds to the idea that types of ultra high frequency waves or vibrations may well be able to transport messages via thought. This could explain how some animals, including fish, mammals and birds can communicate in unexplainable ways.

No longer is it relevant to label unexplained phenomena as 'mumbo jumbo'. Indeed, groups of scientists, mystics, and students of the paranormal, are forming organisations to pool research in these areas, and trying to explain them in scientific terms.

It is convenient for unexplained phenomena to be described as paranormal but in due course it will be recognised that the paranormal is perfectly normal.

Fifty years ago, the idea that a man in a remote desert region could summon help from a small hand held box via a satellite in space, would have been ridiculed.

Having accepted that humans can convey healing and harmony by thought or prayer, the next step must surely be to study any means of enhancing the distribution of this wonderful power.

To the point of this chapter. Everything points to our being able to convey by prayer, all manner of spiritual support over long distances.

This power of 'charitable thought' could so easily expand dramatically on an international scale and create a more compassionate and infinitely kinder human being.

UNIFYING THOSE DIFFERENT

IN SEARCH OF THE TRUTH about our existence on earth, we should dwell on the fact that physically, humans are all the same with only cosmetic differences. Variations in body features and stature, point largely to different climates, diets and cultures. We are born almost identical to one another, and no one race is superior to another.

But there are throwbacks to cave man instincts, when 'survival of the fittest' required the strong to dismiss the weak without a second thought.

With pure physical strength not being the yardstick anymore, man has come to satisfy his yearning for 'superiority' by harassing ethnic, and racial minorities. It is unfortunate that differing religious faiths have often inflamed these leftovers from a bestial age.

Although pessimists believe that this trend is a natural trait of the animal kingdom and suggest that there is a natural tendency to 'hound' out strangers in our midst, this is not so. Horses and cattle feel quite at home with a variety of their kind and relate most amicably.

Research shows that most people of good heart bear no malice whatsoever towards 'different' people in their midst providing they present no threat to life's enjoyment.

In Britain today, we see regular reports of harassment and violence shown towards ethnic minorities by white young males, although the vast number of us are appalled at this behaviour. The young people who perpetrate these deeds are themselves the victims, but that is a separate problem (refer to chapter entitled, Reversal of the underclass trend).

Examples of good harmony between the races take place every minute of every hour and do not reach the headlines. Such news is not considered exciting enough to report.

I relate a situation in the last great war when huge numbers of American troops were stationed in Great Britain. Coloured USA soldiers were stationed in West Row, Suffolk, a remote country area where even people from the adjoining county were treated as foreigners. At first, they felt totally alienated, but when drinks were bought all round at the local pub, and they joined the locals in darts competitions, there was a transformation. Before long, they were made to feel welcome and were accepted as 'one of them'

It is all about finding what people have in common, rather than highlighting the differences.

But today, real efforts are being made in multiracial communities to harmonise relationships. One local radio station actively supports a 'togetherness' programme. The following impromptu conversation, heard on Radio Bedfordshire, was most encouraging.

A cross section of the local community were invited to have an informal chat on the air to discuss their attitudes and feelings towards each other. All their voices were London accented, irrespective of the fact that their parents came from countries, as far away as India, West Indies and Pakistan. They were second generation Britishers talking about their cultural problems. They were not academics or well educated, but their conversation was brim full of common-sense and tolerance. Here were some typical comments,

"I don't believe I am better than you because I am Christian, and although you believe in something different from me, so what! You're just as good a person as me, and perhaps even better", much laughter all round.

A comment from another. *"I think everyone should be able to believe in what goes best for them, and nobody should try and ram religion down our throats"*. Noises of approval were heard.

Another commented, *"These fanatics are a real pest. They get people all worked up to hassle those who don't believe in their own ideas"*.

Another spoke, *"All of us are sitting here friendly like together. Some of us don't understand God I believe, but I think we all believe in something we can't put our hands on, perhaps a super God or something which loves us all. We are all God's children aren't we?"* What can we learn from this conversation?

Here we have people of different races and religions agreeing to their differences amicably. It was noticeable that they were all women, and one wonders if the female gender will be the driving force for peace in the next century. It has been said that women from all ends of the earth share common spiritual values, more so than their male counterparts. Because mothers are the child bearers, they seem to value making peaceful overtures in contrast to males who are inclined to display a macho image just as though humility was a sign of weakness.

But second and third generation ethnic groups are finding it easier to fit into a multi-racial society. Their parents must accept their original culture will be diluted, albeit they may have well enriched the Western culture in the process.

Religious dogma can be compared to party political activities when 'authorities on the subject' are giving us a variety of 'expert' advice about what is best for our well-being. Since they cannot all be right, it is not surprising therefore, that some people distance themselves from God altogether !

An Agnostic, for example, is a person who believes it is impossible to have an accurate knowledge of God. He or she only believes in things of a material nature.

A Humanist on the other hand, can be classed by some as having a moralistic faith, in so far as, whilst he or she rejects the existence of a God, the importance of being humane, civil, and kind, is of paramount importance. It is thought that it is education and not a 'spiritual drive' which guides humans to better things, but since we have had hundred of years of education, the human race should by now be living in perfect harmony!

What about Heathens? This label is applied to someone who expresses disbelief in anything. However, the Oxford Concise Dictionary describes a heathen as being anybody who is not Christian, Jewish, or Islamic. Since two thirds of the world's population, profess to hold beliefs other than those three, the word heathen could therefore be most insulting to a Sikh, a Hindu or a Buddhist.

Returning to the nonsense of racial and religious discrimination, I sincerely believe that all humans have a deep-down wish to accept people at face value.

The philosophy of Positive Spirit aims to build upon this base to create harmony and universal goodwill.

We have much to do and we have the means to do it. What are we waiting for?

GOD, THE UNIVERSAL POWER SOURCE

LONG BEFORE the appearance of humans, simple cells, created from electrical and chemical reaction were multiplying and becoming 'thought generating'. It seemed that cells were learning, thinking and becoming 'ambitious' to change and improve their lifestyle from day one.

The subject is so mysterious that scientific explanations by those experts who should know, get over the problem by expressions, such as 'nature is able to adapt etc. etc.,' or 'it is natural selection which does this, etc. etc.'

To those who deny the existence of a spiritual element, I challenge them to explain within the fields of chemistry, physics and biology alone, how a billion complex forms of life have developed.

At a purely physical level, scientists are making huge strides in understanding DNA, genes, and the secrets of microbiology, but there is a growing humility in scientific circles about the actual sources of life and it is becoming impossible to explain it all in purely scientific terms. There is more credulance now about a master super intelligence, but the terminology of 'divine power' is so unscientific that few use the expression and it is never scene in scientific papers.

Astronauts viewing the Earth and the stars out in space, all claim to feeling a spiritual power, something bigger and more important than their existence.

The mysteries of life, mind, and spirit, are like a jigsaw puzzle, which can never be completed, because more parts turn up daily, along with more spaces to fill. Examining the different parts too intently, creates that tunnel vision which distorts the appraisal of the whole. It hinders the viewing of how all the parts of the puzzle fit together to get at the truth.

One thing seems clear, the gift of 'self improvement' has been given to God's creatures, enabling them to update their own lifestyle and development. Waiting for God to help us along is like a farmer needing water for his crops. He impatiently waits for rain, but alongside his field is a river just waiting for an irrigation channel to be dug. The solution and the power to solve it has been provided by God, but it is up to the farmer to complete the job.

Since we have been given the 'spiritual tools' to transform ourselves into kindlier and more caring human beings, there is no time like now to set things in motion.

ONCE UPON A TIME

THIS IS THE STORY which began in a London maternity hospital, where two mothers had given birth to two boys on the same day.

The two infants lying in two identical cots looked like two peas in a pod. Even their names were similar. One was called Ibrahim, the child of Moslem parents and the other was called Abraham, the son of Jewish parents.

When the parents came to take them home, the staff nurse handed them to their respective mums, or so they thought! You see, that morning there had been a bomb scare and there was some confusion, resulting in nursing staff being over stressed. The trainee nurse had not taken the usual meticulous care, and besides, the names of the two babes were so similar, weren't they?

Ten years had elapsed, and it happened that the two mothers met at the local swimming baths with their children, who were playing together. They shook hands and compared notes. The Moslem mother said to her Jewish

Different worship... one spirit

Ibraham Abraham John Rachel Jonathan

A slight mix-up at the hospital

Mrs Solomon Mrs Hamid

Something wrong somewhere. .... Confusion!

One spirit one family

friend, ' how strange that your boy is so tall when you are so short. Is your husband tall?' , 'No, he is shorter than me!' The Jewish mother said, 'isn't it odd that your lad is so short, when you are so tall.? Is your husband short?', 'No' she replied, 'he is taller than me'.

The truth dawned on them with all the enormity of their discovery.

At first, there was confusion in both families, and they prayed for guidance. They searched for mutual bondings between God and Allah, and the more they looked, the more they found. Gradually, the two families reconciled their problems. The children grew up happily, for each of them had two mums and two dads to love them.

Furthermore, it led to a remarkable friendship between two families of different religious faiths.

There is a moral to this story, which should be recorded and available in every book shop. The title being, 'A short guide to fraternity'.

But for the grace of God, Allah or whatever, you or I, could be born into this world, Christian, Jewish, Hindu, Moslem, Sikh, or Buddhist and so on. The differences between us all, are really man made, and not God made.

We all have arms and legs, and hearts.

We all feel the same pain, love and sorrow.

I stand by my case for a new sensible philosophy, spiritually based. It is that we are all God's creatures and should love and respect each other as one human family.

Now is the time to put this into practice!

Part Three

MEDITATION - A POSITIVE SPIRIT SPRINGBOARD

THE MEDIA TELL THE STORY. We in the West are, for the most part, engrossed in our hunger for achievement and power. We shut ourselves up in our 'own little world' rarely stepping outside and looking in on ourselves to see the logic of our self-imposed worries and stresses.

But the need for tranquillity is being forced on us by the pace of modern life. People are beginning to question 'what's it all for?' and 'am I truly happy?'

There is recent trend of thought which suggests that constantly trying to better oneself to gain more material benefit, has reached its peak. It is called 'downshifting' and refers to those people moving to a simpler lifestyle in the country to find their true happiness. John Crowe describes this in his Fringe-Dwellers manuals, as "minimal living".

More popular is the practice of 'turning off the stressed mind' and seeking temporary tranquillity by forms of meditation, something that has been practised in China, India, and generally in the Far East for thousands of years.

Yoga, in particular, is now taught in all major towns in the UK. The state of tranquillity it can produce is difficult to describe, but for those who are tensed up for any number of reasons, it has an effective healing element.

Practitioners of Yoga also recommend numerous physical exercises to correct bodily imbalances to improve health and mental well-being. But the calming effect of meditation enables problems in life to be handled quietly and in a philosophical frame of mind.

However, there is a knock-on effect beyond the conventional mind/body healing process. Yoga encourages a benign wisdom or a philosophy for living. This in turn leads to caring more about the fundamental issues of the world rather than purely selfish material gains from it.

Meditation is also being used as a healing medium for harmonising the faiths of the world. The British Meditation Society has created a 'symbol of light' which encourages the essential unity of all faiths and love for humanity. Their symbol is shown on th following page.

This is all fertile ground for those intent on taking up the philosophy of Positive Spirit and indeed, those who seriously practice meditation, find they slip into the PS fold quite naturally.

Note. Address of the Yoga Centre in the UK is listed in Index.

Shown on right. Symbol of British Meditation Society.

PRAYERS FOR PEACE

THE PHILOSOPHY for injecting Positive Spirit into a disturbed world, utilises a number of means to spread peace and tranquillity.

Although millions of people are unable to physically help the world with it's numerous problems, no-one should underestimate the effect of prayer. Its power does not confine itself to any one religion, and if you are sincere with wishing to use your soul to spread loving tranquillity, then you need not be religious at all in the conventional sense.

The same applies to those needing help and who turn to prayer in desperation. It only needs sincerity and expectation that comfort, help or guidance will be forthcoming. Out there 'someone' will react to those prayers.

Many thousands more are shy or embarrassed to admit the effectiveness of prayer, as it sounds so 'unlikely' in a world demanding scientific explanations for every phenomena.

But there is gathering evidence that thoughts can actually travel and heal over long distances. It just requires faith, confidence and loving intent. In due course it will be officially recognised. Who knows?, a hundred years from now, 'positive thought healing' could be available on the NHS!

There is an organisation which invites Prayer for Peace with a motif style symbol, called Time Clock for Peace. It calls for everyone at 12am to pray for peace, irrespective of the time differentials. A prayer is said each day by countless thousands of people who are thus linked to a mass "healing session".

Naturally, one can pray at a time and day of one's choice, and many do so, but the effect of 'spiritual healing forces' en masse, is thought to be the most effective method of healing minds in conflict.

Have you noticed how warring factions and political tensions are 'saved' by peace loving people who arrive on the scene and defuse explosive situations?

Prayers for Peace has no formal links with any single denomination or faith, and yet it is used in churches, temples, mosques, synagogues, schools and in individual homes throughout the world. They have been translated into more than forty languages. Such prayers can be latched on to any religious faith, or become part of the faith itself.

The surest contribution anyone can make to world peace, is to realise peace in his or her own heart, and feel the urge to share it!.

If you would like to be part of this venture, it requires only a simple commitment to the daily discipline of remembering the prayer of your choice, when it will automatically link itself to that of many others around the world.

One suggested prayer goes like this :-

Please let my peaceful thoughts join others.
To spread love from one person to another.
To give compassion to all beings in need of it.
To send joy and serenity to all beings.

Another prayer goes like this:-

Lead us from death to life, from falsehood to truth.
Lead us from despair to hope, from fear to trust.
Lead us from hate to love, from war to peace.
Let peace fill our heart, our world, our universe.

The above peaceful prayers are suggested versions, but if you have a feeling to 'put it another way', the only proviso is that the prayer should convey peace, love and compassion between all humans and governments.

Just as a billion rain drops produce a raging current, so your little prayer along with thousands of others, could give peace and harmony a boost beyond one's wildest dreams!

'ONENESS' IN THE EYES OF BAHAI

EVERY RELIGION has it's merits in the eyes of the believer, so it is unfriendly to debase another's faith, but such is the blind loyalty aroused by dogma, rarely do the faithful of one religion have anything good to say about their 'competitors'.

There is one exception, so it would be remiss not to mention a relatively unknown faith which differs from the normal concept of a religion, because it expresses remarkably similar ideas to those within the Positive Spirit Philosophy.

In the late 19th century, there was this wise man from Persia, a Mr Bahaullah. He expressed his faith and wisdom in letters to heads of states, including Queen Victoria.

The basis of his progressive ideas was that all humans should religiously strive for world peace and universal brotherhood. Followers of this admirable concept formed a religion called the Bahai faith.

The significant difference of this faith to other religious orders, is that it did not seek to create disloyalty by suggesting that people should abandon their faith, and join the Bahai. But it preached that we are all God's creatures and should join forces, as it were. The ultimate purpose being to bind all humans in peaceful coexistence mentally and physically.

The problems for attention in the world, were accurately described, and here is a summary of some Bahai writings which still apply to these modern times:-

Nationalism
Where groups of people feel the urge to forcefully impose their will on others

Poverty
Excessive poverty relative to excess wealth
When wretched suffering and hardship create unacceptable injustices.

Racial and ethnic intolerance
When people will not accept their 'different' neighbours as human brothers.

Religious fundamentalism
When religious dogmatists impose their religion on others and excite persecution.

Political confusion
When religious countries released from tyrannical regimes become frustrated, negative in outlook and extreme in behaviour.

But the followers of Bahai are optimistic of the future and believe that such problems as described above, will surely be overcome.

They describe the future as 'undone.', and believe all countries will live in global peace, following a super effective United Nations.

Optimistic statements include:-

'There will no longer be vast differences between rich and poor countries. Every child in the world will be able to go to school. Everyone will learn a world language so that we can all understand one another better. Women will be treated equally with men and they will use their influence to help bring about peace in the world'

The Bahai faith is worth investigating. It is brim full of good sound philosophies of the loving and caring kind, and can be incorporated into one's own religion, if one has a mind for it.

The philosophy of Positive Spirit is very much in accord with the Bahai concept of a new age to come, but there is only one feature missing, they omit to describe how souls will develop in order to create that predicted harmony of the human spirit!

Could it be that the PS philosophy which in times to come will be incorporated within networks of light, and be one means of completing that spiritual path, which Bahai and others are predicting?

PART FOUR

GROWTH POTENTIAL FOR POSITIVE SPIRIT

SOULS IN ACTION

'TAKE MY CHILD and give her love. I cannot feed him. I have no husband, no money, no nothing!'

These were the words of a sad peasant woman who deposited her child at the front door of an orphanage in Romania.

This is not fiction, but reality as told by a member of a team of volunteers, who returned recently from a mission in Romania.

It all started in August 1991, when Mr Leo Lacy heard about the plight of thousands of orphans living in miserable conditions. Their sad plight came as a result of the policies of the former dictator Ceaucescu, who banned contraceptives and abortions for increasing the population. This created a desperate plight for mothers, already desperately poor, who were unable to feed their children.

Leo Lacey was inspired to search out for volunteers to organise and arrange convoys of goods and services to travel to various orphanages, refurbish them and if necessary, rebuild them.

Amongst one group of volunteers, was a heating engineer and his wife, Mr and Mrs O'Donohoe. The reports of the conditions there, spurred them into action. Not only were the orphans, aged 7 to 17 years, deprived of the love and care from parents, grandparents, uncles, or aunts, something we take for granted, but living conditions there were pathetically inadequate.

Souls in Action

'Presco'

Food, toys and clothes
for orphanages in
Romania

'Let's-Go'

Mr and Mrs O'Donohoe took it upon themselves to organise a convoy of trucks full of building materials, food, gifts, and clothes. Their aim was to refurbish an orphanage in Bucharest, which had fallen into bad disrepair. A handful of valiant staff there were trying to look after 200 orphans living in semi-squalor.

The orphanage had long since run out of government funding, and was becoming uninhabitable.

Food, clothing, and equipment were in very short supply, and the building was in desperate need of repair. The plumbing and sewerage system had broken down, and there was no one to attend to it.

When an SOS for volunteers and equipment was made to support this project, 'Romania with Aid', the response was overwhelming. Volunteers came from all walks of life and included bank clerks, housewives, secretaries, along with plumbers, decorators and electricians. They freely offered their services with a number giving up their holiday to join the venture, but the O'Donohoes had a problem. They had the helpers, but money to buy all the things required had not materialised, so they put an advertisement in the Watford Observer. Now comes the miracle, which shows that beneath the hard crust of many business people, there lies hearts of gold.

To their astonishment, they were deluged with building materials, trucks and unlimited fuel. Local supermarkets and traders offered food, clothes, toys and toiletries, all free with no strings attached!

A month later, a convoy of four trucks and helpers left Watford for Romania, and two months later, the orphanage had been transformed and refurbished to a reasonable standard. The children, some of whom, had never had toys of their own, learnt how to laugh and be genuinely happy for the first time in their lives.

The main point of this true story, is that almost all people have compassionate feelings which they can rarely fully express, so when the opportunity arrives, the soul works overtime and there is a crescendo of loving generosity.

It all goes to prove that there is an enjoyment in helping others in distress and this is the key which can open a floodgate of Positive Spirit on the world.

Part Four

POSITIVE THOUGHTS

* At present, decisions made at soul
level, are pushed down the 'priority
queue' in our scramble for success at
any price.

* Just as a sprinkling of acorns give
birth to a forest of oak trees, so
caring ideas in fertile minds are the
seedlings for a compassionate
world.

* An adult's character is only as good as the environment surrounding his
or her childhood.

* Let us wake up to the fact that the world is but one country and mankind
is it's citizens!

* Before we leave our world, should we not say, 'thank you', and put
something back into it, so as to make it just that little bit better than when
we found it?

* The media is focusing only on the world's problems, not the solutions to
those problems, and we are mesmerised by what is not working, rather
than what is!

* If you receive love, you will find yourself giving it to others. If you
receive hate, your heart will breed the very same negative feeling, and
you will be hateful. Be first to create that positive cycle. It will catch on
fast!

* We are part of something bigger than ourselves, and we should not be shy
in reminding ourselves of this fact, when power and possessions seem to
be so very important.

✳ When you do a kind deed with no advantage to yourself, your spirit is going positive, and your soul abounds with exhilaration. Just try it and see for yourself how it works.

SELF-ESTEEM IN OUR HANDS

DOMINANT CHARACTERS often command the scene and receive a disproportionate amount of respect, in contrast to passive personalities who are inclined to feel inadequate without any real justification.

'Go getting' style characters are generally hungry for power and easily get hooked on it. But often they get tense with ambition and are not really happy people in their search for new heights of achievement. Unfortunately, they become inconsiderate to others in the process.

In a world where dominant opportunists tend to prevail, there is a need for more quiet thoughtful people with positive aspirations. They provide the balance to offset the negative trends of power hungry industrialists and politicians.

We all have varying degrees of dominance and passivity in our genes and these traits are housed in two areas of the brain. The left side is masculine, ambitious, analytical, intellectual, and demanding. The right side is feminine, artistic, intuitive, holistic and sentimental. For instance, sergeant majors, police warders, boxers, and karate enthusiasts, enjoy assertive behaviour, but musicians, poets, artists, dancers, and philosophers, portray a softer nature.

But almost everyone has a balance of these qualities and there are a number of grey areas. At times, even quite caring people show aggressive tendencies when emotion and stress swing their behaviour patterns.

But spirituality is primary seeded by sensitive and intuitive people, expressing a quiet healing wisdom of the spirit.

We should therefore qualify the value of success and check whether that 'go getting' person has the balance necessary to make holistic decisions.

An inventor of a car that reaches two hundred miles an hour in seconds is honoured by the industry, but not by ecologists who see the danger of more pollution. The boss of a successful supermarket chain who makes village shops bankrupt in the process, is blinded with a false sense of achievement.

But what is the message then for those who feel unworthy with low self esteem, who perhaps cannot land that job because of loss of faith in their ability, who feel intimidated and do not possess that drive and confidence they see in others?

It is this. Be proud and reject all notions about your inferiority. Your value to the world is immeasurable, because it is gentle, non-aggressive and caring people like yourself who compulsively express peaceful aspirations. But this does not mean you should abandon developing a degree of assertiveness, because your good nature will be more effective with a little bit of "go" behind it.

You are a needed person, so feel good about it!

From interviews with genuine 'travellers', rather than dropouts and criminals who have gone mobile, they are people who see a new enlightened age, spiritually based, and free from the artificial and materialistic based one of the present age. These are not drug and rave people. In some ways, they emulate the early USA settlers, who in the last century were looking to start a new life, New life...New age?

The last movement towards new thinking was in the 1960's, when 'peace and love against war' were expressed by young people. This was an expression of their rejection of war-mongering super powers. But they also rebelled against authority in general, which reflected in raves, drug taking and disorder.

We can now see that in all social upheavals, self-discipline must be maintained because the vast majority of us need to lead orderly lives.

But this is a phase, not any permanent trend towards anarchy. My optimistic note is based on a number of hopeful signs coming from unexpected sources, some of them controversial.

The aspirations of those who see the Aquarian Age or New Age, vary somewhat, but they have some basic common ground. They all predict, promote and encourage positive spiritual values. These can be summed up by expressions of universal love, justice, and caring. Such sentiments are not new of course. Positive values encouraging the brotherhood of man have been talked about for centuries, introduced into religions but too infrequently practised.

But light workers, as they are called, are projecting their belief of an enlightened age, when humans will have resolved their differences, and live together in harmony, goodwill, and mutual understanding. This is not, as some might think, just idealistic fashionable thinking. Light working groups are spontaneously popping up across the world. They are sincere people without profit motivation.

No question of a cult or a religion arises, because they believe the prophets who founded the various religions, were all sent to "show us the way to live", rather than be martyred and idolised.

BOMB MAKER WITH A SOUL

BOMB DESIGNERS are unlikely to have highly developed souls, and because of their preoccupation with destruction, are considered to be devoid of any compassion. But this true story shows that the most unlikely people have soul developing potential which can burst into life and transform their negative horizons to positive ones.

But why is anybody designing bombs of mass destruction in the first place? It points to spiritual instability in an age of advanced technology, a rather dangerous combination!

One explanation is that holistic considerations are overwhelmed by the excitement and ego satisfaction which material achievements give.

Inventions such as electricity, radio, motor cars and atomic bombs, can all be classified together as products of man obsessed by creative achievement. The value of the products to man's progress is overwhelmed by profit, politics and giving employment. Morality and wisdom take second place.

Even brilliant scientists with the highest IQ can lack both common-sense and sensitivity. Some have feelings of grandeur when they 'play God' to beat nature at its own game. This can be lead to dangerous situations.

Part Four

To illustrate this point, I quote from the memoirs of Sakharov, that eminent nuclear scientist and designer of Russia's hydrogen bomb.

'I felt like God regenerating the mysterious energy of the sun and stars. I felt unbelievably excited. I had the ultimate instrument of power within my grasp'.

But thankfully, there was a spiritual transformation of his character, when he realised the horrific implications of his discoveries.

Strangely, he could not explain how he had received 'messages' to stop his work and oppose the development of such devastating weapons.

For this unpatriotic step, he was banished to a Siberian labour camp where he suffered terrible hardships.

This intelligent and remarkable man further stated in his memoirs; 'I was initially inspired by emotion rather than intellect, and patriotism clouded my moral judgement'.

This true story brings to light the confused state of human thinking on the world scene, when a few people with exceptional intelligence can bring humanity to the brink of annihilation.

There is an added moral to the Sakharov story, because having awoken to his true peaceful role, he devoted the rest of his life to human rights causes in a most fervent way.

One can only theorise how the spiritual element came to enter Sakharov's soul at a crucial time for the world, because his thoughts changed dramatically from 'destruction' to 'construction'.

There are strong beliefs that we are entering a new age of spiritual consciousness, when holistic values will dominate human decision making. But in the meantime, we must monitor what we do with our technology. Intelligence without the guidance of a spiritual philosophy, is like a train on a journey with the signal man taking a day off. It is Russian roulette of the most hazardous kind.

Positive
Re-think!

Bomb maker
with a soul

Part Four

HOLISTIC AWARENESS FOR BOSSES

THE TITLE OF THIS CHAPTER might conjure up the image of a company director seated at his desk with a little halo around his head, a symbol of angelic innocence. But people running businesses are no better humans than members of their workforce. However, they have a special responsibility, because the way they conduct themselves affects the lives of those who work for them.

During daylight hours of consciousness, people in employment often spend three quarters of their living time at their place of work. The conditions and environment in the workplace therefore have a profound effect on the minds and moods of those people.

I have had an advantage to judge these matters first hand, having spent half of my working life as an employee and the remainder as an employer.

Life as an employee, first on a farm and then with a building company, could fill a book but it provided an insight into the value of job satisfaction and going home in a happy frame of mind. Furthermore, it enabled me to put some theories into practice.

Observations showed that low morale usually comes from bad management. This often comes in the form of overbearing managers who, being under pressure, resort to bullying tactics often quite unintentionally. The unhappiness this creates spreads through the workforce. You see 'negative vibrations' start at the top with the boss and work their way down to managers and eventually to the doorman.

Some might argue that if everyone spoke nicely to everyone else, it would be a sign of weakness and discipline would suffer, but in practice this rarely happens. A business can be run with a minimum of coercion if the staff have been trained properly and know what is expected of them. It is a question of inspiring self-motivation and giving praise when it is due, and not harping unduly when things go wrong.

It is all about an holistic approach to managers and employees alike, not forgetting the boss. You see, 'director managers' at the top often become unstable when they drive themselves too hard. So often, they take their problems home with them and find themselves working ninety or more hours a week. In such a state, they become obsessed with wealth and more often than not, stressed with the thought their business will fold up if they relax for a moment.

Naturally, we all value a good living standard and the means of acquiring a few luxuries, but once obsession takes over, a soul destroying process takes over and wealth becomes pointless. Marriages break up and health often suffers.

Many women and men go to work to escape loneliness, not merely for the income, so it is essential to recognise the need for a happy environment. The idea that people take advantage of an easy-going atmosphere is usually expressed by managers unable to gain respect without resorting to demanding tactics.

Time and time again, I noticed that if instructions from management were given in a courteous manner, they were respected and not taken advantage of, as some would believe.

Employees should be regularly asked if they have suggestions and made to feel part of a team.

You might query where 'holism' comes into the picture. After all, it could be viewed that a good staff relationship is just common sense. But harmony in the office or factory has much wider implications.

Most of the miseries of the world are caused by ignoring the plights and problems of others. If people can train themselves to 'step into the shoes' of opponents, disputes even wars can be defused at source.

Likewise, the holistic aspect of life in the office and factory, lies with the feelings of goodwill, happiness and respect people have for each other. But the holistic element does not rest there. Tradesmen and visitors to the premises sense and absorb ' positive vibrations' without realising it and, when the staff go home, they take their 'vibrations' back with them. This permeates into the home atmosphere and spreads to other members of the family.

Summing up. If each of us realise we have a part to play in making our 'local world' a happier place to live in, who knows whether this trend can catch on and reach out into the world at large!

In the meantime, where better to do something positive than in the work place?

Part Four

LAUGHTER ON THE NHS

A PSYCHOLOGIST who has studied the effect of laughter supports a growing belief that, in this modern world, we would all thrive on a special tonic, but not one from a bottle. It is literally childish fun and games. You see, childish silliness and fun, in which most of us indulged, remains in our subconscious mind and ready to be released when the occasion arises.

When you feel under pressure and wound up, a splash of humour is also a safety valve. You become less edgy and more reasonable.

In this book, I have continually emphasised how the experiences of childhood are reflected in adult behaviour. The 'childhood effect' on the adult, has it's lighter sides. A child's train set motivates a grown up to fill his attic with a lattice work of railway lines. Indeed, the happy experiences from childhood are part of our education, vital for a friendly disposition and an outgoing personality in later life.

On the negative side, many of us work under pressures and the problems of the day are inclined to be 'mountains', when in reality they are 'molehills'. It is when we become mildly neurotic and irritable that we have a duty to ourselves and others to 'let rip' with childish irrational laughter to bring us back to rational thinking once more.

Laughter, too, is a tonic for those depressed, morose, and distressed, and has a clear therapeutic value. The motto, should therefore be, to laugh regularly and encourage a sense of humour amongst all those you encounter, especially those who look unhappy.

Worries can be reduced to mild problems with laughter when they are then found to be manageable.

Laughter is like adding 'icing to the cake' in the general effect of feeling good, but it also has a genuine healing value in the physical sense, because a substance called endorphin in the brain is stimulated and this gives to the body's immune system, a 'repair and mend' effect.

One doctor has already suggested that laughter classes would be a natural tonic for health promotion, and could reduce the country's huge medical bill.

Laughter on the N.H.S. might not sound so absurd as first perceived!

Laughter on the NHS ?

Part Four

SHOE EXCHANGING

ONE HEARS THE EXPRESSION 'If you were in his shoes, you would do the same'. This implies that if you could train your thoughts to suppose you were in the position of that other person, you would be more sympathetic with his or her problems.

But at present, there is a low PS threshold, and the 'shoe exchange' mentality is at a low ebb. In the strive for achievement, the ego suppresses spiritual impulses, so that one's horizon centres on one's own 'little world'. This attitude is seen in most spheres of life, particularly in warring factions when the participants are like zombies.

Did a Serb stop to think. 'I might have been born a Croat if God had made it that way! Just what am I doing with a gun in my hand? His 'spiritual mirror' did not reflect the absurdity.

What about that group of youths taunting that young Sikh about his turban. Do they ever stop to think what a commotion, their Mohican haircuts would raise amongst a group of young Indians in the Punjab?

Further examples of spiritual insensitivity are, muggers who cannot imagine the pain of their victims and racists who fail to dwell on the misery they cause. Bomb droppers are totally remote from the terror down below. Drug traffickers do not feel the hell of the addicted.

But the people who commit such criminal acts, would be the first to campaign against them if their family were at the receiving end of the crimes. Only then, would their souls spark to life , and consideration given to changing lifestyles..

Although the above are extreme cases, consideration for others applies to every facet of life. When it enters the political arena, it is also has a healing role, because when governments can 'feel' the predicaments of other countries, and visualise their problems as though they were their own, there is a tendency to extend goodwill with peaceful gestures.

I therefore have a message to all those who are about to take up arms. Think on this, 'by the Grace of God, you could be in the shoes of that person you confront with hate in your heart. Therefore consult your soul, turn off your hate, and make peace with yourself'.

The philosophy of Positive Spirit is brimful of common-sense, along with the spiritual values it promotes. This is just one of them!

Think if you were in his shoes

Bradford - England

Punjab - India

Part Four

THAT UNSELFISH TREND

THE REPLACEMENT of selfish attitudes by more caring ones on a universal scale is an immense task, but I am optimistic. Positive trends can catch on fast and no better example is our growing awareness of 'human rights". A hundred years ago, positive action to protect the rights of an individual in another country for humanity's sake, would have been unthinkable.

Therefore, once the PS philosophy has become absorbed into societies, it will become self creative and eventually become the norm for holistic behaviour across the world.

But first we need to reverse the negative trends of modern society. This requires us to revalue our latent spirituality in two ways.

First, we need to spread an awareness that we all have a valuable 'spark of God', waiting to be used. Then, we need to build a confidence for exploiting this wonderful gift for the good of humanity.

'Kick starting' positive values into the adult world population who are heavily polluted with negative ones, requires a complex range of ideas, all perfectly feasible and described in other chapters. But planning spirituality for the next generation and beyond, involves young children who can better absorb holistic values at an early age before the soul destroying hype of the adult world has taken root.

Happily, the seed of the PS philosophy has already been sown in the primary school by the green movement and the love for wild life, which portrays nature's wondrous variety of animals and plants. Extending this love into human nature is an obvious progression, and it is good to see that a start has been made in bringing the world's problems into the classroom. Already, children are getting involved in sponsorships to raise money for such projects as digging wells, and alleviating starvation in third world countries.

The aim is to plant a subconscious thought within the minds of growing children which says, 'I must do something for the world when I grow up' This will have the effect of creating an unselfish trend in their characters and as they mature they will be more thoughtfully in tune with holistic ideas to solve the world's problems.

There is no implication that young people must become religious or develop a missionary spirit. They have numerous other matters on their minds in adolescence. Sexual awareness, with all its traumas, and the problems of finding employment largely occupy minds at this difficult period in life. But with a healthy outgoing soul, there will be an element of caring built into their characters which will shine out in numerous ways as they go about their life.

People 'primed' at an early age with Positive Spirit make decisions with inbuilt holistic considerations quite naturally.

Without doubt, education of the type that feeds the soul nurtures the seedlings for world harmony.

Note. Education of the soul is dealt with in depth within the chapter entitled, What now education? There is now an organisation called Peace Child International which encourages children of all countries to meet and create peaceful initiatives.

WHAT'S THIS LOVE ALL ABOUT?

The word, love, has different meanings for different people at different times, so a summary of its variations may help to unravel the confusion.

Love, which involves motivation to gain fulfilment, can be broadly divided into two sections.

* An expression of enjoyment including sexual gratification.
* Affection of a platonic and unselfish nature.

Love involving enjoyment can vary between being totally benign and downright evil, but affection is almost always benignly positive.

Love for possessions. Most people aim to have a good standard of living which involves earning as much money as possible. If it involves supporting a family, and the earnings come from an ethical source, this style of 'ego love' is reasonable. Should a person adopt criminal means to attain his wealth, his love becomes highly egoistic because he is prepared to hurt others to obtain it. But love for material possessions, whether obtained honestly or otherwise, does not always bring happiness, strange to say. Wealthy people are shown to be the least content, and even some lottery winners have regretted their windfall.

Love for sporting activities. Whilst we may take up sports merely to keep fit, there are others whose self-esteem requires them to live dangerously during the process. They will claim they just enjoy the excitement and challenge, but risking one's life on purpose climbing dangerous mountains, shooting the rapids in a barrel or sailing round the world in unstable little boats, are trying to prove to themselves that they are important. It is almost certain that in early life, they have been humiliated into feeling unworthy and they are fighting back, even being prepared to endanger their lives in the process.

Top people in sport are driven to succeed, partly by the financial reward but also by the need to be appreciated. One only has to see how scorers of goals, gesticulate in pride to the supporters on the football terraces. It is admiration which 'turns them on,' as the saying goes.

Everyone needs to prove by some achievement that they are worthy of respect, and sport is a positive outlet for this purpose. But in an inner-city environment young people may become hooked on negative outlets for their self esteem, and their peers applaud their unlawful achievements. The goal scorer who revels in the admiration from the terraces is replaced by the joy rider racing down the high street in a stolen car, who seeks admiration from his peers.

Sexual love. This is an instinctive desire for orgasm provided by God to perpetuate the species. If it is shared equally with a loving partner, it is a caring form of love and promotes harmony.

Lustful love, on the other hand, without tenderness, is egotistical and will be soul-destroying if it becomes pleasurable for one partner at the expense of the other.

One 'leggedness'
goes positive

Helpful to
receive

More pleasing
to give!

Pornography can so easily become a drug, when excitement for sexual fulfilment demands all manner of stimulation and unhealthy practices.

Platonic love. This is an unselfish love, which stems from the cradle and is the most crucial type of love. It has its roots in the love which a mother feels for her newly born and has a spiritual quality too!

Here is a replica of a human being... your very own. It is there within your arms alive and kicking.

The platonic love within a family group, (irrespective of whether it is a one-parent or two-parent one), is only selfish in respect of the inclination to limit it to the 'personal family' and not the 'human family' outside. This is instinctive and reflects a deep-down insecurity about the possible intrusion from 'those outside'. Breaking down this protectionism by encouraging soul enhancement on a grand scale is the challenge before us.

The main philosophy behind the PS movement is to find every possible means of extending platonic love by creating an enjoyment for camaraderie across all boundaries, social, racial and geographical.

Love of camaraderie. There are many grey areas of 'platonic love' built into our social structure. One is a love of togetherness, expressed in people enjoying each others company and is typified by gatherings in the pub, on the dance floor and social clubs.

But there are negative sides to camaraderie. For instance, groups of people drawn together from insecurity or fear will swear 'loving' comradeship and allegiance to each other. They need bonds of friendship with those of like minds to feel strong and are prepared to resort to violence in support of their cause. This is camaraderie of the inward looking variety, in that whilst a loving fellowship can exist within a group, its activities can be harmful to those outside it.

The author belongs to Compassion in World Farming whose members are of one mind and feel strongly about factory farming, but the camaraderie goes sour when a few members become violent to another animal, the human one.

If you examine disputes without prejudice or favour you may spot that the people on both sides are basically reasonable people, but their interests differ and there is no 'mechanism' on hand to resolve problems peacefully. The pressure for a solution often comes from exhaustive war and the misery which stems from it. But that 'mechanism' can be found by adopting 'holistic lateral thinking' and using it in positive ways. Here is an example;

A landowner in India who rented out field allotments to poverty-stricken peasants to meet his own debts, was involved in serious confrontations with his tenants. The peasants had no capital and few facilities to grow enough food to sell and reduce their own mounting debt. But an enterprising bank working alongside horticultural experts, agreed to make loans at low rates of interest to groups of peasants who were persuaded to form co-operatives and farm efficiently. They adopted more productive methods of husbandry which included using night soil from the city for composting and rotation of crops to increase soil fertility. Within two years, several hundred communities of peasants were making a profit, paying off their debts, increasing the productivity of their plots and providing a good supply of vegetables and maize to sell in the town market.

Love within the PS philosophy. This is really an extension of platonic love but more vibrant and enjoyable: It should not be confused with an evangelistic style of expression, which is too forceful and narrow in concept.

You may ask just what are the special qualities of this 'super love', which will bring all humans together? Firstly, it is an outward looking and unselfish love. It is more unconditional and contains three Cs,...Caring, Compassion and Consideration for others, when no personal gain is sought after. This may be difficult to achieve in practice but it is the ultimate target for tranquillity in mind, body and spirit.

Some people's self esteem is so low that they need to prove to themselves that they have that "inner sensitivity" on which PS can prosper.
Your television screen has shown painfully thin starving children with desperate pleading eyes penetrating yours.

Did you feel upset and a desire to help in some way?

Part Four

An old woman describes with emotion the scene in a church during the last war. It was filled with 300 women and children who had taken refuge there. A bomb skidded down the church steeple and landed in the vestry without exploding. They wept in thanks to God. It was thought to be a miracle. No one was hurt.

What is your spiritual reaction to this happening? Did you feel the emotion of thankfulness and relief for those people?

An earthquake in Turkey creates urgent need for twenty thousand blankets. People were asked to kindly donate one blanket and send it to a certain address.

You didn't do so. Did you feel slightly guilty?

By now, you will have realised Positive Spirit is the type of love, which feeds the human spirit. This love surmounts all barriers of race, colour and religious divisions, and is crucial to our spiritual evolution. It requires no doctrine or law to enforce it, can grow indefinitely and can become a human instinct if encouraged to do so.

This is the love that really matters, and with an inexhaustible supply of this Godly power source, which I call Positive Spirit, the future of the world, as we know it, lies in our very own hands!

Peace Child - Earth Summit 92

Part Four

OUR SENSES, TODAY & TOMORROW

ASK SOMEONE to list the human senses and most will say, touch, smell, taste, sight and hearing. However, the Oxford dictionary has more to say on the subject. It mentions sensitivity, common sense and a sixth sense. But there are other senses, What about love, instinct, intuition and telepathy?

One instinct stands out amongst others. A newly born child, kitten or calf, having fed from it's mother through the umbilical cord for months on end, will instantly reach out to drink through the mouth.

In humans, the maternal instinct to hug her new offspring, is accompanied with joy, combined with wonderment and gratitude for the divine power of creation. This is an instinctive sense which is truly the source of our spirituality!

Carl Jung, the eminent physiologist spotted this instinct and proclaimed it as an aspect of spiritual dimension, and the basis of the human soul. At a seminar of psychiatrists, a leading speaker summed up this theme very well. He stated, "Western man's most urgent need was to rediscover the divine element in its being, which was illusive and often ignored". He continued, "there was a danger that in our profession, that we were cutting ourselves off from the spiritual forces, leaving a world which recognises only mind and body".

The above exposes one more sense, the Spiritual One, which is common to all healthy humans across the planet without exception.

This spiritual sense which can be described as soul sense is fed by an inexhaustible supply of divine power. In the past, it was believed that animals other than humans were devoid of souls, and not fit to be treated as sentient beings. This is reflected in the ill-treatment of animals which persists to this very day.

It is clear we have some way to go before we can say humanity has reached spiritual maturity, but we can help the process along by supporting the precious sense of... caring, compassion, love, justice, and respect.

SPIRITUALITY AGE... ON ITS WAY!

WE ARE LIVING in an age of transition which commenced at the turn of the century but came to the surface in the 1960s. The cold war was at its height and young people were rebelling against traditional restraints. Since then, seventeen African nations have become their own masters, and small wars across Africa, Middle East, India and Bosnia continue to appear. Traditional religious worship is losing its appeal and more women are at work than men. Casual sex is commonplace and the nuclear family is under threat.

It might seem to some people that the world is falling apart because change is disconcerting, and we feel more comfortable with predictability. But the situation could be compared to a country just released from a repressive but orderly regime, when people become disorientated and cannot handle their new found freedom. Order has been replaced by a worrying disorder, and people feel insecure about what the future holds.

If there was nothing to replace the apparent disorder we see in the world, then indeed, anarchy would be on the horizon, but the media brings our attention to negative news at the expense of developments which rarely reach the headlines.

Positive ideas and organisations are springing up, largely not reported by the media. To give support to this view, I have listed a number of organisations, some sponsored by offshoots of the UN, others initiated by charities and people who have felt the need to 'serve the world' in some capacity. But this listing has only scratched the surface of a growing expression for healing and helping the world along happier paths.

* **New charities** are being formed at an ever increasing rate, estimated now at approximately fifty per week in the UK alone. Many of them are manned by unpaid volunteers. Offshoots of the United Nations, such as UNICEF, are continually being formed to make the 'talking shop' of the United Nations more meaningful.

* **Volunteers Overseas.** Thousands of young people are now working overseas in a voluntary capacity to alleviate hardships in the third world.

Arms of Compassion

✱ **Peace Child International** has a prime mission to create a bond of togetherness between all young people from different countries. They meet and communicate to discuss and share their problems. The ideal is based on creating a harmony of goodwill and working in unison to rectify injustices, poverty and threats to the environment.

✱ **Radio for Peace** is sponsored by the World Peace University. It beams peaceful initiatives and news across the world 24 hours a day.

✱ **Rescue Mission... Planet Earth** is an offshoot of Peace Child International. It has a global action plan for the 21st century, and has an educational trust which involves all young people from different countries working in unison to improve the environment, fight pollution and promote the cause of peace and understanding between all peoples.

✱ **Peaceful Global Consciousness** is mounting pressure on the arms industry to switch to peaceful employment. A new inspiration is created by a quotation, 'every warship launched and every rocket fired is a theft from those who are not fed, housed or clothed'.

✱ **Earth Summit** saw the largest ever global gathering of civilised societies. It brought together 400,000 people from 18,000 organisations and 172 countries, who were all searching for solutions to the world's problems.

✱ **Global Co-operation for a Better World,** formed by 60 dedicated visionaries at the United Nations, are actively pursuing peaceful solutions to the world's problems.

✱ **Human Educational Curriculum.** Costa Rica is the first of many nations to adopt a Human Education curriculum in schools. This instils in children the ethics of respect and concern for other beings and all forms of life.

✱ **Interfaith India.** In August 1993, a meeting was held between representatives of four interfaith organisations; International Association for Religious Freedom, the World Congress of Faiths, the Temple of Understanding and the World Conferences on Religion and Peace. The theme of the meeting was 'visions of interfaith co-operation in the 21st century'.

* **Global Forum 94.** On-line now regularly circulates information to all countries about sustainable development and mutual assistance on such matters as economics, agriculture, poverty and conservation of resources.

* **United Peoples Partnership for Peace.** (CAMDUN). This is a United Nations offshoot and its role is not to just rely on world states to initiate justice, peace and goodwill, but to establish an ethical code for peoples across the world at 'grass roots level'. Such matters as 'teaching peace', sustainable development, disarmament, and micro investment to help raise living standards, are just some of their activities.

* **Global Net Trust.** A newly formed trust to train young people to create positive media, hold an optimistic vision for the future and promote positive activities to support these aspirations.

* **Positive News** (Planetary Connections) is a positive and holistic magazine/newspaper which is now read in over 80 countries. Its purpose is to link up and spread news about peaceful initiatives and ideas to further harmony across the globe, a valuable link-up medium for bringing peaceful initiatives into fruition.

* **World Harmony Through Service** is a universal focal point for all those wishing to serve the world in some capacity or other. It wishes to provide a beacon of inspiring light for sparking the souls of people who have thought about helping the world but have not quite got round to doing anything about it.

* **Findhorn** is a teaching and meeting centre in Scotland which encourages a world culture based on holistic and spiritual consideration for others.

Residential and workshop facilities are in Forres, Scotland. (Details at end of book).

✳ **Mori poll of 1995.** This showed a striking rise in young people rejecting materialism. One in five interviewed seemed to reject it, but in 1970 only one person in twenty did so. Such people were more caring and conscious of the environment.

✳ **Light Working International Centres.** There are Light Working Networks in most countries of the world. There is no question of a cult, sect or religion within this spiritual network: Light workers are spiritually inspired people and express themselves outside conventional divided religions. They describe their work as serving the light. and their numbers are rapidly increasing as it appeals to all those with visions for a better world with a common belief that peace, love, compassion and goodwill will ultimately prevail. They believe all sincere people can become inspired 'messengers' and collectively, also individually, call on Divine Power to harmonise people, defuse conflicts and spread universal fraternity.

IT IS IN OUR HANDS

*WE HAVE BEEN GIVEN
POSITIVE SPIRIT TO
HELP HEAL THE
WORLD*

THE WORLD NEEDS HARMONY

*LET US FILL EVERY
CORNER OF IT WITH
THE HARMONY OF
LOVE AND JUSTICE*

SPIRITUAL FOOD FOR CHILDREN

BIRTHING SPIRITUAL VALUES

FROM WHERE do spiritual values originate?

The very source of compassionate love, and the caring element is an extension of the instinct expressed by the natural love and adoration a mother feels for her newly born. "Education" is meant to sustain this special love from there onwards but continuity has not materialised. Some like to blame karmic influences, but this is a negative stance and feeds the pessimist's view of mankind's future. By and large, the newly born starts off on a level playing field. The trauma of birth, together with the circumstances and health of both mother and child, will naturally have a bearing on the emotional state of the new arrival, but this applys across the board. In essence therefore, the character of a child at birth is unblemished, irrespective of ethnic origin, geography or status.

The urge to hate, envy, hurt, steal, kill or be cruel is not just yet within the thought field of the unborn child, but from birth the sponge effect of the young brain picks up every imaginable aspect of human life. No spoken word passes an infant's lips to denote that he or she is being 'educated', but the 'seeds' of character and soul take shape from the first minute of arrival and many believe from the moment of conception.

Here is a message for the mother-to-be. Start loving your baby once you realise you are pregnant. It can feel the spiritual warmth of love you generate and this is the 'spiritual food" on which the child will thrive.'

On the physical plane, eat healthily, avoid smoking and go easy on the alcohol. Avoid stress and be happy!

Prior to the childbirth, study and practice relaxing exercises, but my role is not to emphasise methods of childbirth except to suggest that natural ones are preferable.

It is not generally realised that the actual birth is both painful for the baby as well as the mother, and soothing gentle handling is needed.

It is quite a shock for a baby to leave a cosy warm protected environment in the womb and following a painful delivery, be smacked to 'bring it to life'. Immediate separation from its mother can also add to the trauma for a new young life. Both these procedures are gradually being phased out for there is now a strong belief that personality problems are sown even at this very early age. It should be remembered that at birth, the child is really nine months and one day old, and the brain cells are already beginning to feel, think and store information in an extraordinary way.

Even if the child is born out of wedlock and adopted, it will sense if it is wanted and thrive spiritually if it is shown love and caring interest from a person other than its mother.

As the child grows up, school can become an extension of the caring process, and not an end to it. Just as children now project close feelings for wild animals, trees, cats, dogs, rabbits etc., so these green tendencies can reach out to include closer feelings for the human animal kind in all its splendid variety.

Nursery school should be an extension of "mother stimulation", but if there is a lack of affection and stimulation at home, it may need to be a replacement for it.

Within the school syllabus, the concepts of caring, compassion and justice can be introduced in ways which will foster peace and understanding between people of different race, colour and origin. Ways to do this without imposing extra burdens on the teachers, are described in the chapter headed 'What now education?'

The philosophy of Positive Spirit has the means of steering children in these positive directions but it also requires the co-operation of local communities, religious institutions and close ties between parents and teachers.

Children's books should all have a 'message' within the stories, expressing in subtle forms how universal love and service to mankind can be as exciting as fighting pirates and Red Indians.

Young souls can be compared with seedlings confined to a flower pot where roots are restricted. Green fingers then plant them out and expose them to light and rain in fertile soil, so they can flourish. Like young plants which need nurturing so do the souls of young children need all the love and attention they can get, but in an environment of fair discipline and justice.

The children of the world dictate the future harmony of the world and this fact should be in the forefront of progressive minds.

WHAT NOW EDUCATION?

FIRSTLY, a message to the 3 Rs supporters. The philosophy of Positive Spirit is based on creating good human beings who can relate peacefully with each other. All else is of secondary importance.

Currently, education is directed towards excellence in reading, writing and doing sums, thus enabling school leavers to obtain employment and lead fulfilling lives. This priority exposes fragmented thinking.

If the art of human relationship is missing, namely, the means of harmonising relations between one human being and another, instability is inevitable, and that it what we see across the planet.

Official views on education show two schools of thought, both of which are short on vision.

The 'progressives' believe the need is to encourage the personal expression of the child with knowledge for its own sake being of secondary importance. The 'traditionalists' see the prime need of education as being the acquisition of knowledge.

The philosophy of PS leans towards the 'progressives', but it is obvious that one cannot fill our modern world with lovely people all doing their own thing, but who cannot spell or put two and two together. Their creativity would be hindered.

Common-sense should tell us that a combination of the two concepts is needed but I go one stage further; there is a third aspect of education. It is the soul enhancing element which every child needs so more holistic use can be made of the knowledge intake. Thus, a well-balanced holistic society needs people with a blend of all three concepts.

Children naturally need knowledge to be able to express themselves on a variety of subjects, but in these troubled times we need creative people and holistic original thinkers. Young people cannot develop these traits under a 'knowledge at all costs' curriculum.

Even at primary school, children can be trained to question and discuss what they are taught. It is not a matter of rejecting the 3Rs but redirecting them along holistic lines.

Could we not ask some of the older children some minor provoking questions to stimulate their creative thoughts?

∗ *Reading the newspapers, "what do you think is wrong with the world?'*

∗ *"What were the wrong decisions of leaders in the 19th century?"*

To satisfy the need for writing skills they should be asked to write an essay, say, on the lessons we can learn from history and what we should do to avoid the mistakes. Afterwards, each child could read out their ideas, followed by a free discussion. Minds would be stimulated, and a new breed of young people would appear, ones that think for themselves and question their elders about the errors of the previous generation.

The ultimate aim for youths should be to inject into the adult world a new ethos for thinking holistically. This would mean that without hesitation and quite naturally, all considerations would have a built-in core of moral and ethical ingredients, when greed, violence and injustice would become naturally abhorrent.

For example, a chemist excelling in arithmetic would use his knowledge for the holistic benefit of mankind. He would not dream of using his skills for, say, developing chemical weapons, but would be self motivated to research means of removing salt from sea water so vast tracts of desert land could be irrigated, reclaimed and used to feed the hungry. His achievement would inspire others and promote the soul enhancing process which is the backbone of the PS philosophy.

It is so very clear that knowledge without a self-motivated drive to use it to help the world, has been the missing link in the spiritual evolution process. Minds need to be fed with a wisdom primed with an ethos of world caring.

The ills of the world are largely products of what children see, hear and feel from the activities of grown-ups, and, without positive education such as described, there is a downwards spiral for mankind which could lead to styles of anarchy as seen in some 'no go' areas in the USA.

Parents naturally are largely responsible for their children's early character tendencies, so, in fairness to teachers, one must accept that the 'education' of respect, honesty and good behaviour is a dual responsibility.

Should the parent(s) of a child be living in a hostile, deprived area within an atmosphere of violence, teachers will find it more difficult to impart kindly values to their charges, and since such children will one day become parents themselves, determined measures are needed to break this spiral of social depravity which is carried forward from one generation to another.

Education, as generally envisaged, is designed to be character building but if you think about it, the Mafia and drug barons are 'educated' rogues. Conversely, some 'uneducated' people have turned out to be wonderful people. Christians would quote their Jesus, a carpenter, with little formal education, as coming within this category.

On the world scene, with a billion people barely able to read or write, there is a plea that education must be available to all. But is this the prerequisite for harmony and peace? Without doubt there must be a new qualification for an 'educated' person.

The virgin souls of young children, from loving parent(s) naturally show a forward spiritual intent, for instance when they play 'nurses and doctors'. Their caring attitude towards animals also highlights the soul sensitivity upon which we can build.

The sceptics may doubt whether this caring trend can sustain itself into adulthood, but such an attitude treats selfishness as though it was an illness without an antidote.

This key to a nicer human being has been staring us in the face for centuries. It is a question of redirecting the motivations of young minds by gently introducing into the educational system, values of a less materialistic and self-centred nature. These values must be enjoyable and make sense to children hardly out of their nappies. They enjoy love, hugs and being cared for, and learning to impart these considerations to others is a natural sequence which we can so easily encourage. It is a question of self-nurturing caring ideas. One cannot order young people to be kind and considerate. To be effective, it needs to be expressed from within and outwards

The above might suggest that discipline is being abandoned, a claim by those who live by the mistaken theme, "spare the rod and you spoil the child".

There must be a balance. A doting parent, not prepared to exert guidance and fair discipline, will seed "caring for self" aspirations at the expense of "caring for others".

Childish culture is largely based on dolls, train sets, cars, soldiers, and now, electronic games. These early fascinations create trends in later life. For instance, the cult of train enthusiasts, who fill their lofts with railway track, can trace their passion from happy childhood days playing trains. The same applies to collectors of model cars, dolls, toys, cigarette cards and toy soldiers. These were the joys of their childhood days.

If a fascination for human fellowship can be slipped into young minds at a very early age, there is every possibility that a new generation of caring adults will emerge. There is a need for the fascination which 'trains sets in the loft' bring to the nostalgic adult, to be replaced with 'my favourite charity'

How do we set about this?

From day one at school, there is a quest to absorb knowledge, to read and write. All this with a view to acquiring a job, getting married, having children, enjoying life, becoming rich and respected. The missing link is the notion that we have also come into this world to make it a better and happier place for others. If one can establish this idea even at play school, children will grow up with positive thoughts, less selfish, and decidedly more caring in outlook.

Children with their multi-racial classmates can already form a bond of togetherness and create within themselves, a sensitivity about the world's peoples and their trials and tribulations. Many teachers encourage this, but before we can make real headway, there are problems to be overcome.

Parents try hard to be good role models, but have difficulty in portraying consideration in a society which obtains it's 'feel good' effect from negative media competing for sensationalism

The problem is compounded because there are thousands of parents, who were themselves "deprived" as children and so positive role models are in short supply. Some teachers, too, have had problems in childhood and find it difficult to express caring attitudes to the children in their care.

Teachers therefore must be carefully vetted and better valued because they have become character builders as well as knowledge providers. They play a vital role in bringing spiritual values into the lives of young minds. This must be recognised by all agencies and given huge support.

If we all had the same religion, soul growth could be raised through a common faith, but religions are in disarray, and compete for followers. 'Unholy' rivalries often contradict the original 'holy' concepts of each respective faith. A One loving God does not emerge when splinter groups violently disagree about the interpretations.

But we now have a multi-racial society, and the problem about a suitable religious syllabus for school children comes up as regular as clockwork. Parents do not like their children losing their religious identity and culture and show a marked protective attitude. Indeed, a minority of parents have removed their children from schools which they consider give disproportionate attention to their particular faith.

The solution to the problem is not to over emphasise any one religion, but to introduce universal ethics as the basis for soul development.

Religious instruction therefore should be portrayed in such a way that children see all religions as being sacred, but with one Almighty God in charge.

How does the overworked teacher tackle the challenge without feeling overburdened with one more responsibility? They obviously cannot cope with this on their own. It will be a case of teachers, parents, school

The 4th R.... Relationships

governors and local communities co-operating, and being inspired to work together enthusiastically in a friendly spirit.

The theme of most religions, namely, *that we should treat others as we would like to be treated,* can easily saturate 'sponge' minds if we give it more priority.

This theme can be subtly introduced into many school subjects; so children can see a healthy moral view of life.

The aim must be to get young children into frames of mind, which are balanced, fair, considerate, loving and respectful. It can start early with the four year olds, and here are some suggestions upon which to build:-

'God made this wonderful world for all of us to look after.
Look at the thousands of different trees, birds, flowers, animals and fishes, all in lovely colours, shapes and sizes'.

At this stage, simple biology facts are presented with supportive illustrations.

'All these wonderful creatures came about because God loved us very much, and wanted us to look after them.
People are very precious too, wherever they live in the world. Because the world is cold in some places, and very hot in other places, people have different colours and habits. Dark skin protects them from the sun in a very hot climate'

At this stage, simple geographical facts are introduced, showing where the temperate climates exist etc. This to be supported by illustrations of living communities.

'Sometimes it doesn't rain for years in some countries, and nothing will grow. People die of hunger unless they get help from people like you and me, who send food by air to the people who need it.
You see we must show our love for people even if they live a long way away. We are all really part of one big family.
Just think, you might have been born in a part of the world where it

hardly ever rains! Wouldn't you think it kind to get help from the lucky ones?
So children, we can all see how important it is to love and help each other. If you are cruel to someone they will be cross inside and be cruel to someone else, and so on, and so on. What happens?..everybody is unhappy!
At the beginning when you were hugged and loved by your mummy or daddy, you felt happy and safe. If everybody felt loved, just think how happy everybody would be!
In this class, and all over the world, children look different. Just like flowers and trees, people too are not alike. Some have a lovely brown or black colour. Some have big eyes and some very small ones..
But children, inside our hearts we are all very much the same'

The following could come within the religious lesson or at school assembly,

'Close your eyes and let us pray to God that people all over the world can love each other and live happily and not fight each other '
' Thank you God, for allowing us not to be hungry, for giving us a bed to sleep on and clothes to keep out the cold'

The younger children happily read stories by Blyton, Milne and Lewis Carrol, but what about stories which inspire kindness, honesty, compassion, respect and caring? It could spark an early wish to see our world in a wonderful light with everyone keen to help each other in their own community or to serve humanity in some way.

For older children, a more clarified theme is needed, on the lines of the following:-

'When you were younger, you may remember being taught to be compassionate and loving to all God's creatures. But now you are becoming important to the world because each one of you has the ability to show your goodwill to others of different races or religion, even if they see God in a different way.
All the main religious groups, Christian, Jewish, Moslem, Sikh,and Buddhist, proclaim their love for the main God which looks down on all of

us.

Just close your eyes for a minute and imagine you could have been born with different parents in a different part of the world. You would have a different colour and you would be trying to master a different language!

Whatever you decide to do when you leave school, try to do just one small good deed each day, and perhaps a specially good deed once per month. Just try it.... you will feel really good inside!

Remember, when you are old and ready to leave this earth, your grandchildren may ask you a question, "Grandad (or Grandma) what did you do to make the world a better place? What are you going to say to them?'

Every human being on earth was once a child, and since caring children create caring adults, so the world's future lies in holistic education.

A SERIOUS THOUGHT. The importance of children is so vital to the future well-being of the country, we should be pressing now for a Minister of Relations. A person responsible for adding a 4th R to the 3 Rs, R for Relations. Without being able to Relate in harmony with other human beings, we become a fumbling humanity with lots of knowledge and unable to apply it with holistic considerations.

NOTE TO PUBLISHERS OF CHILDREN'S BOOKS

Books with a 'global spiritual message' are, at this moment of time, few in number. But the Positive Spirit Network is in the process of sponsoring authors of children's books which portray fulfilling ways of 'helping the world'.

CHALLENGES FACING POSITIVE SPIRIT

SWORDS TO PLOUGHSHARES

THERE WERE QUIET PERIODS in history when swords were melted down to forge ploughshares. With the cold war over, this aspiration could apply to the present day, with guns and atomic warheads being melted down to forge railway lines and civil aircraft, but as the twentieth century closes, we have yet to reach that happy stage.

We feel comfortable with predictability and stability, so the idea of further change can be a worry for some. Inevitably, those who seek change with a new spiritual vision of humanity will meet strong resistance from those who feel content with the status quo.

To assess the situation we need to study the 'darkness' and the 'light' of human development.

The darkness

Humans have not yet evolved that loving spirit of peaceful coexistence and the leftovers from arms stockpiling are sold at knock-down prices to those who would overcome their neighbours by violent means. Since 1945 over 20 million people have died in conflicts.

They have been small wars compared with the 'great wars', but with infinitely more suffering imposed on innocent old people, women and children.

Part Six

One could blame to some degree a certain Mr Kalashnikov, the inventor of a cheap devastating repeating hand gun. No one person can have contributed so much to human misery. A man with a grudge, wielding this tool, can kill and maim as many people as could formerly be done by a company of well armed troops. We have seen how countries like Somalia, Afghanistan, Sudan, Bosnia and recently Albania, have become devastated by the indiscriminate use of these guns and others like them.

The destructive power of modern weapons have changed the dice. In the 18th century, nine out of ten people killed were fighting men, but in the 20th century, the same proportion are civilians.

One would have supposed that each new century would make us more sensitive to the misery of settling conflicts by warring. Not so. One person, previously armed with a sword, could only kill one person at a time, now he presses a trigger to mass-destruct at a distance, without seeing the faces of his victims or hearing their cries.

In an aeroplane, the tilt of a lever can kill thousands within seconds. The pilot does not think, 'my God, there are mothers and children at the receiving end of this!' It is the utter remoteness of 'seeing the kill', which dulls the sensitivity and removes the remorse and responsibility.

It has been said that if modern man had to resort to wielding a sword like his ancestors, and look into the eyes of his adversary in battle, he would more readily seek a peaceful gesture. It is certain he would have refrained from killing civilians so blatantly.

Following the 1000 bomber raids on Dresden during the last war, British prisoners were made to help clear up the carnage. The brother of the author was one of them. On one night alone, 30,000 men, women and children had been killed, many being burnt by flash-fires caused by mass incendiary bombs. The horrifying sights of charred bodies gave the prisoners nightmares which time never healed.

Comments from the arms dealers go like this, 'we sell arms to countries for their defence and to deter aggressors' or 'we fulfil a service' or 'if we didn't sell them arms, somebody else would'.

The arms manufacturing industries unfortunately give vast employment, so politicians ignore the unethical aspect of producing tools of death. At this moment of time, arms factories are the biggest employers in the Western

Challenge for PS.... 2000 AD

Mindless arms!
Legless victims!

world, and without their export revenue there would be wholesale bankruptcies and disastrous unemployment. But disaster is only relative, and the suffering caused by modern weapons has been an unparalleled disaster for the human race.

Technology with all its brilliance has yet to be matched by sensitivity and sensibility, but we should not despair for the future of mankind. There is now remarkable evidence that changes are on the way, albeit we shall be well into the 2nd millennium before the benefits of the 'light' come to heal the disquiet in human relations.

The light

There are numerous signals of holistic trends out of sight to most of us, for it is the exciting and negative things which are drawn to our attention by the media.

We are bombarded with sensational news and intrigue and rather like a drug, reason and quiet contemplation become rather boring. In such an environment, positive news rarely meets the criteria to excite.

Yet positive concepts and aspirations are prospering behind the scenes and the expression 'New Age of harmony' becomes more meaningful when one checks out the positive peaceful trends on the horizon.

Already there is a ground swell of contempt for the volume of small arms, mines, and weapons being sold to countries who could so easily settle their differences amicably. By the year 2001, arms factories and predator dealers will, by international law, be switching from destructive products to constructive ones, this being sponsored by the UN and peace agencies. This will be enforced by governments on their arms industries.

Even at this present time, autocratic governments with poor human rights records are being ostracised, often with sanctions being applied to bring them into line. It follows that within the next decade or so, justice and democracy will become a signature of pride and will become the criteria for respect and acceptance by the vast majority of nations.

The arrival of Nelson Mandela from South Africa heralded an astonishing excitement. Millions thronged the streets to welcome a messenger of peace, love and forgiveness. He forgave his former white tormentors and told others to leave go of their hate, and shake the hands of their enemies. People loved the man. He was not preaching, just speaking from his heart. Like Gandhi, Martin Luther King and the peacemaking prophets before him, Mandela sowed a seed of loving fellowship which is the food of the growing soul.

Without doubt, a lasting peace will eventually arrive in Northern Ireland, the Middle East and even Bosnia, where racial hate seems endemic.

I visualise a new revitalised spiritual New Age when people will overwhelm those who hesitate in settling disputes amicably. No longer will such matters be left purely to reluctant governments with other priorities.

Before the end of the 21st century, I am most optimistic that settling disputes by war will be seen as both obscene and barbaric.

I can visualise museums of 2500 AD, displaying some of our war artefacts with inscriptions, 'samples of man's inhumanity to man, pre-New Age period... Late 20th century.'

DEPRESSION NEEDS THE POSITIVE

A MILDER FORM of depression could affect you should your husband be made redundant, and your baby go down with measles simultaneously. If all this coincides with the lawnmower breaking down, there is every reason to feel under the weather. People who are depressed, see life as being worthless, unenjoyable, and in extreme cases, unbearable. It can be caused by post-natal depression or the menopause.

But more often than not, depression is brought on by loneliness or situations which create a feeling of hopelessness when everything looks bleak and miserable. Furthermore, a person in that state does not believe anything can be done about it.

There are several antidotes. One effective one, is to imagine you live in a country with little food, no medical facilities, no electricity, no plumbing, with washing done at the river's edge.

Dwell on this scenario for a few minutes, and then open your eyes. You might well be asking yourself, 'what have I got to be depressed about?'

A man who lost his legs in an accident, was distraught and considered suicide, until he joined a club of legless people. The world showed a friendly face once more!

Lonely people who have lost a loved one are very inclined to be depressed and feel unwanted. The secret is to become involved in your local community, perhaps joining clubs, or groups doing voluntary work. There is little time to feel sorry for oneself if one is involved with others, supporting needy causes.

There is a further remedy for depression which involves powers of the spirit, when desperation has been reached. It involves praying earnestly for help and if you are a just cause, it will arrive in some form within a few days or earlier.

You see there is a Spiritual Help Line into which you can tap for assistance and if you are religious, pray through your faith.

Christians have an advantage, in that the PS concept is built into many of the teachings of their religion, and divine help can be drawn in more effectively. But make no mistake, when people are desperate for help, and it is deserving, help will surely arrive in some form, perhaps in unexplained ways, but come it will.

The more faith you have in the power of the benign Positive Spirit, the more effective is the remedy.

The PS philosophy seeks to cultivate universally this divine power to help the frail, the needy, and yes, the depressed!

CRIMINALS OR VICTIMS?

INTERPRETING CRIMINALITY in all its forms requires us to check our emotions and think both logically and holistically. This is something which many people have difficulty in doing, because the natural reaction to swarms of flies in the kitchen is to spray them dead. The idea of checking what attracted them into the kitchen in the first place is overlooked in the passion for removing those dirty flies.

When it comes to criminality, the problem is more complicated because a criminal in the eyes of one person can be perceived as a hero by another person. To come to logical conclusions, it requires us to shut out all preconceived views on the subject and start from scratch.

Who are the criminals? At the top end, we have dictators, war criminals, drug dealers, the Mafia and planned terrorism. But what about the polluters of the sea, the land and the air we breathe? The latter group can be the most devastating, yet since they are unintentional, they fit into a separate group classed as 'international negligent criminals'.

At the lower end, we have thieves, muggers, fraudsters, shoplifters, arsonists and hooligans.

Now, imagine you are in a maternity hospital and, before you stand rows and rows of cots exposing little bundles of new life, as yet untarnished by the adult world. Your thoughts are interrupted by a security guard keeping a sharp eye on his charges as his casual remarks have shocked you out of your spiritual contemplation, 'what a shame so many of these little darlings go astray, sweet innocents one minute, little devils the next'

What can we learn from this? It seems to suggest that the future of every child is a lottery, or that its future is mapped out in advance by God or the Devil, something over which parent and community have no control!

Naturally one cannot predict how one's child will turn out, but it is nonsense to infer that we cannot deter children from lives of crime.

In chapters entitled, 'What now education?' and 'Reversing the underclass trend', I have described in detail various means of tackling crime at source, but briefly, we need to study the atmosphere to which our children are exposed at a very early age. If children are 'served up' with anger and a range of violence and abuse without affection, then they are 'marked for life' as potential criminals. Should they have a dominating nature, they will be aggressive in their anti-social activities, with hooliganism, 'road rage' and racial attacks being some of the milder consequences of their abused childhood. But should they have a gentler nature, they will be prone to mentally illnesses, become alcoholics, or drug addicts.

When parents have themselves been deprived of a positive lifestyle, their children are at a disadvantage from day one.

The truth is unpopular but everything points to 'criminals being victims' in addition to the 'victims of the criminals', and, if you can deal with the source of criminality, you are helping potential victims most effectively.

There must be many progressive thinking people who agree with this reasoning, but acting upon it remains difficult to accomplish. There are several reasons for this. One is the emotion aroused by a 'mob addicted public' towards crime. Any suggestion that the cause should be dealt with rather than the symptom is stifled by suggestions that the criminal is being favoured at the expense of the victim. In effect, every time a serious crime is reported in the press, the government curry favour with the electorate and react in a knee jerk fashion, stating, 'we will come down harder on criminals' and 'we must build more prisons' and 'we will not go soft on crime'.

One recent headline in the press stating, 'lock 'em up for good' echoes a scenario in Paris when onlookers shouted 'off with their heads' as the guillotine did its ugly work.

In Spain, the crowd roars for the end of the bull, but in truth, the Matador and his supporters are the criminals and the bull has committed no crime whatsoever.

It all seems to show that snippets of the primitive savage still inhibit the soul enhancement process. But there are examples, on occasions, which contradict this view. When an old lady was recently brutally attacked by a teenager, a mob attacked the police van in which he was being driven, but the lady when interviewed in hospital, was recorded as saying 'he must have lost his mind to do such a thing. His family must be so upset at their boy's behaviour'. Here was a case where the victim had recognised the instability of the perpetrator and queried the cause of the crime rather than the crime itself.

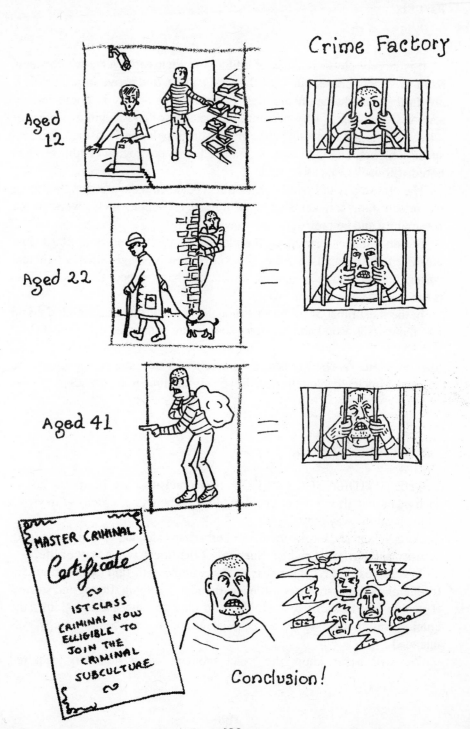

Crime Factory

It is largely physical abuse of children in their early years which steers them to violent crime, but once they are caught, and arrive in prison, they are further caught up in the web of criminality. This is borne out by statistics which show fifty-percent of inmates re-offend within two years of release. It is not surprising that the prison population is rising. Inmates spend long hours in their cells in cramped, soul destroying conditions, and bored with lack of positive outlets.

The philosophy of Positive Spirit directs that from the moment they enter the prison door, inmates should be trained for employment, work in the community and be prepared for a new life.

But on a longer term basis, the plan is for all children from playschool onwards to be brought up in a positive environment, taught what is right and wrong, encouraged to be compassionate and have respect for others. This is the key to a crime- free society.

In the meantime, dwell on this thought, 'but for the grace of God could I be that person who had the wrong start in life and ended up in prison?

Special Note. Ways to tackle criminality within our inner cities are described in the chapter entitled 'Reversing the underclass trend'.

THE CRUELTY STREAK

THE HISTORY BOOKS SHOW how cruel we have been, not just to each other, but also to the animal kingdom. Where does cruelty come from and is it on the way out?

As cavemen and cavewomen, our barbarism extended to killing for food, security and territorial rights. 'Survival of the fittest' was a way of life.

In those early days there was a desperate need to find explanations for frightening things, such as pestilence, thunder, lightning, floods and storms. If people had to sacrifice a child on an altar to 'appease the Gods', the cruelty was thought to be a 'necessity', and no deliberate cruelty was intended.

We will never know the exact moment when humanity acquired

compassion and sensitivity, but thoughts of consideration for others have slowly crept into our thinking and reasoning.

People who suffered cruelties began to hesitate before imparting the same treatment on others. This could have been the seed of compassion which sparked the spiritual saying 'do not do to others that which you would not wish to be done to yourself'. Nevertheless, the caring and kind traits of humanity are still very frail and the media remind us of this on a daily basis.

People still succumb to powerful oratory and if they have a grudge against their 'neighbours', can behave with utmost cruelty. No better example of this was the tribal slaughter of thousands of Tutsies by their neighbours, the Hutus. 'Instructions' had been given over the local radio to destroy every 'rat' in their midst with promises that God would reward them with happiness.

But humans are not universally bad, and alongside their cruel streak lies a saintly quality. For every person classed as evil there are at least ninety-nine who are basically compassionate, fair minded and reasonable.

A survivor of the holocaust told the author, after being asked if he now believed in God, 'my traditional belief in God has left me, but I see an unlimited spiritual goodness in people and that is where I see God'. As a young teenager he was hidden from the Nazis by compassionate people for several years until he was discovered. He then experienced a year of horror before rescue came in 1945.

His experiences within a concentration camp, commanded by deranged people, were devastating. Groups of people, devoid of compassion, were plentiful at that time, and their evil doings disgraced humanity. Yet, the genuine warmth of love and support he received from those hiding him and from large numbers of people following his release, reassured him that there was after all. spiritual love and compassion within the hearts of most people.

As the second millennium closes, we can truthfully say that although cruelty appears at regular intervals, the majority of countries are now actually concerned with the plight of innocent victims of aggression and persecution wherever they appear, and are prepared to apply sanctions and involve UN troops to protect innocent victims. The most recent example of 'cruelty consciousness' was in Bosnia in 1993, when the barbaric treatment of Bosnian Islamic civilians by Serbian Christian soldiers shocked the world into action.

The United Nations, at this moment in time, is still in the process of coming to terms with it's peace making roles, but one can recall a resolution was swiftly passed to rescue starving Kurd families stranded on mountain sides in Iraq. UN Soldiers, elite in their trained role for killing, were brought literally to tears by the scene which met their eyes during their mercy mission. The pictures of misery on the faces of young children had sparked their souls with compassionate feelings. The question of different culture, race and ethnic background was of no consequence. The world had cared and was prepared to act upon it!

We now have every reason to be optimistic because over a minute period of 60 years, which is a blink in the evolutionary time scale, we are witnessing groups of nations making compassionate gestures in unison.

True, we still have cruelties in drug culture, ethnic violence, and Mafia style crime, but these are leftovers from human self-destructive tendencies. They are not approved by the majority of countries and 'positive' education involving 'soul enhancement' will squeeze out these evils at source.

I prophesise that in our grandchildren's lifetime, the cruelties of the 20th century will be considered as barbarism of a bygone age. Do we not now show the same disdain for our forbears, who burned witches, tortured unbelievers and sent little boys up chimneys a century or so ago?

Without question, that 'cruelty streak' will wither in the face of overwhelming compassion, but we must have optimism in the better nature of mankind and encourage it to prosper.

Optimism brings hope
Hope is the embryo of creativity
Creativity brings reality to fruition

ANIMAL COMPASSION AT A PRICE!

OUR COMPASSION level is especially fragile when there is gain or advantage involved. This is highlighted by our attitude towards animals. The more endearing ones, like dogs and cats, get VIP treatment and the law comes down hard on those who mistreat them. But when it comes to farm animals, a veil of callousness descends on some of us when we shop in the supermarket. The following 'less than comic' strip illustrates how we 'sell our soul' in order to save 10p on an egg and 50p on a chicken.

'Lock up your cat in near darkness for weeks on end in a confined space of 14" by 12" by 12" and you are a criminal of the lowest order!"

'Lock up your dog in near darkness for weeks on end in a confined space, 18" by 12"' by 12" and your hate mail piles up !'

'Lock a chicken up in a small cage in semi-darkness along with four others, each space allocated being 12" by 9" by 9", and you save 50p on your Sunday lunch'.

Part Six

All warm blooded animals feel the same pain and stress as we do and we are hypocrites if we claim to be animal lovers and allow these cruelties to continue.

Join **Compassion in World Farming** and exert the utmost pressure to have factory farming made illegal (address in closing pages).

TRANSFORMING THE EGO

FROM THE NAPPY STAGE we are all on the mildest form of 'ego trip' because the essence of wanting to 'live life' is to enjoy what life has to offer us.

An egotistical person might be classed as somebody rather selfish and self-opinionated. This need not be so, because we can get an 'ego fulfilment' from giving pleasure to someone else. Putting it another way, one can get pleasure "within oneself" when portraying kindness or compassion to another person. This might be termed the 'ego of the soul' when fulfilment is obtained from "self-reward"

Ego in all its forms plays a star role in the way humans behave, and just being introspective about one's own behaviour can be productive.

On the political stage, people can get carried away by their ego, and introspection becomes vital to prevent leaders blundering into aggressive stances without foreseeing the consequences.

Let us list a range of egos to put the issues in perspective and to show the diversity of subjects which give people a 'buzz'

Artistic/Creative Egos
Music, painting, singing, poetry, sculpture.

Entertaining Ego
Disc jockey, compere, comedian, film star.

Sporting Ego
Marathon runner, tennis star, mountain climber.

Negative Ego (acceptable)
Prison warder, sergeant major.

Negative Ego (unacceptable)
Terrorist, bank robber, war criminal, drug trafficker.

Positive Ego
Social worker, doctor, fireman.

Positive holistic Ego
Publicly recognised... Priest, Rabbi, and Mullah.
Often unrecognised... Charity worker, Light worker and all spiritually inclined organisations and people who work for peace, love, compassion and justice in all its forms.

Whilst the above might suggest we have fixed paths for our egos, we often change in mid-stream and human nature comes up with surprises.

There are feminine patterns which guide us along more sensitive and peaceful roads, whilst male ones, of the more 'get up and go' variety, take us along more aggressive routes. But we all have both male and female tendencies, easily recognised when we see a female all-in wrestler at work, or a male ballet dancer in Swan Lake.

Transforming egos on the world stage has brought transformations of the human psyche beyond our wildest dreams. To name a few:-

Former terrorist Menahim Begin became prime minister of Israel and was awarded the Nobel Peace Prize.

Nelson Mandela, former head of a terrorist organisation, spent 27 years in prison, yet on his release forgave his tormentors and was ultimately elected prime minister of South Africa. His expression of love and peace for both his people and former adversaries were universally welcomed. In consequence, he has become a role model for healing racial divisions with powers of influence likened to Martin Luther King and others before him.

Ego 'tripping'

Climbing up
mountains
for pride

Harmless

Climbing up
houses
for cash

Souless!

Negative Ego.... Respect from war making

Positive Ego.... Respect from peace making

Part Six

Summing up the implications for 'changing the ego'.

If so called 'evil' people can be motivated to become almost 'saintly', it suggests a resolution for the rest of us.

Every dispute, whether it be in the home, in the work place or in the political arena, can spark two searching questions:-

Is a peaceful solution sincerely my main interest?
Am I prepared to lose face by compromising?

PART SEVEN

REVERSING THE UNDERCLASS TREND

THE UNDERCLASS CHALLENGE

WHY UNDERCLASS? The word 'underclass' suggests a worthless inferior group of people to whom we have no obligation. What an arrogant stance to take about fellow human beings who have been disadvantaged through circumstances beyond their control!

The crux of any challenge is a strong desire to meet it and beat it, and what better way to get to grips with the underclass challenge than first remove any notions of conceit relative to the class structure. But it does require us to think laterally and dwell on the thought that you or I might have entered this world in the form of a dog, a bird, a goat or lizard, and very possibly, a child in an underclass family.

So if each of us had been less fortunate with our own personal circumstances, we too would be in a minority, struggling to find our self-respect and having to contend with a 'worthless' label.

The expression 'it could have been me if God had willed it' is an edifying thought and becomes a reality in the event of the death of a family member from an incurable disease. Following such a personal tragedy, we often support research into a cure for that illness so others have a better chance of survival.

It is all a question of identifying our purpose in life and whether we can find a niche in our busy lives to alleviate the misfortunes of others.

But to reverse the underclass trend will require a total commitment of numerous agencies, as in a wartime situation. This time 'the enemy' is the breakdown of human dignity and a precious caring element which should be there to support it.

Abused children. There are numerous interpretations of abuse in the context of abused children. There is physical punishment applied in anger or premeditated, and there is sexual abuse when the perpetrator has usually been similarly abused in childhood. But there is also mental abuse, the effect of which has been totally underestimated. Few realise that, in the early years, even humiliation, unfairness, and aggressive language in the home can have far-reaching effects.

But at source level, the subculture arises from a number of failings in our social care and education system.

Society has lost sight that human instability originates from the 'sponge mentality' of young minds who log every negative experience. If they are tough enough, they will 'climb out of misery' and join their own kind in a camaraderie of rebellion, but, if they are of a frail nature, they can suffer in silent misery. Should this seem to be an imaginary fear, think again. The charity Childline recorded last year 20,000 telephone pleas for help. Since it is estimated that three out of every four children are too traumatised or afraid to make a telephone call, the number of children suffering verbal, sexual or physical abuse in a violent household, is a horrifying thought.

Dietary factor. There is also a relation between diet and behaviour which cannot be ignored. For instance, it has been shown that many hyperactive children can been cured by changing to a wholesome diet. It would not be out of the way to suggest that some of the 'hyperactive' hooliganism on the football terraces has a dietary connection.

But what about the parents of the hyperactive? A 1995 poverty report states that thousands of pregnant women on income support were unable to afford a healthy balanced diet. Yet many manage to feed their family in a most commendable way, albeit doing without some of the luxuries others take for granted. Nevertheless, there are mothers often not really knowing what is meant by healthy nutrition. This exposes a vital need for education on the subject.

One hindrance to healthy eating is the vested interests of the food industry consistently plugging quick-fix junk foods. It is therefore essential that young mothers should receive positive dietary and health education as forcefully as the TV commercials.

Meeting the challenge.   There is a variety of reasons why human deprivation needs drastic attention. We see what is happening in the United States, where community inertia has created huge ghettos of misery and crime. British inner-cities are already a microcosm of those in Harlem. Like Canute expecting the sea to stay put, we chat and stare at the problem and expect it to right itself by righteous talk and stop-gap solutions.

On the present basis of our piecemeal approach to the problems, we shall be no more successful than our American cousins in reversing the underclass trend.

Relying on governments to address the problems of our inner cities has been a disaster and the challenge now needs to be met by the people themselves within communities. The social services and community care agencies will be playing their part but the initiatives and enthusiasm will come from within each community with thousands of volunteers coming forward to play their part in restoring pride to their neighbourhood

But before detailing the means for them to adopt to meet the challenge, it requires us to examine the problems and the unfortunate people whom we are trying to bring back into the fold of positive living;

* Inadequate parents with low family morale.
* High unemployment spawning negative outlook.
* Abused children who create a chain of perversity.
* Racially-harassed people living in trauma.
* Deprived families in run-down neighbourhoods.
* Aggressive children from unloving parents.
* Malnourishment, affecting health of mind and body.
* Drug pushers, creating criminal activities.
* Teenage vandalism motivated by boredom.
* Parents who portray negative role models.

* Inadequate housing, lacking social amenities.
* Alcoholism and drug-addicted people.
* One-parent families unable to cope and provide.
* Drug related crimes and violence.
* Children with behaviour problems within schools.

My aim is to show that the human spirit can be motivated to handle this immense task. It is a question of 'activating the Positive Spirit ' on a grand scale when goodwill and enthusiastic co-operation will be the key to success.

Stop Press. Just prior to this book going to print, the new Prime Minister, Tony Blair, has formed a government unit to 'Rescue the Underclass', described as a great social issue of the 20th century. Central government on its own cannot achieve this goal, but the next chapter, entitled, 'Reversing the underclass trend' describes the means of doing that very thing.

SCENARIO FOR CHANGE

IN THE LAST CHAPTER I listed the deprivations which have created a sub-culture in many inner city areas of Britain and some estates bordering our towns. Before establishing a plan to rectify the immense problems, it is necessary to dismiss the argument that it is just poverty that creates an underclass. There are billions of poor people in the world often leading more contented lives than the wealthy whose possessions become more of a worry than a joy.

It is deprived poverty which needs our attention because we are talking about people deprived of a meaningful living quality.

If young people are denied positive outlets of expression they will latch on to negative values and get fulfilment from "achievements" of the same kind. This is reflected in hooliganism, drugs, theft, truancy, graffiti, and a camaraderie of gang violence. When they become parents themselves they find their own children ensnared inside the same ghetto world and those on the "outside" are seen as the "enemy".

To extract young people from this sub-cultural web is not easy and as we approach the next millennium there is a need to wake up from our lethargy and face the challenge with optimistic intent.

The cycle has to be broken and our children given the chances they deserve! But to kick-start the means of doing this requires a special motivation, namely, a bond of true commitment of purpose from social services, schools, the general public, charities, central government and buoyant enthusiasm from the local community. But it will be the people with their spiritual empowerment and confidence to succeed who provide that dynamic driving force.

TARGETS FOR SOCIAL HEALING

✱ Involve children intensely in positive pastimes.

✱ Improve the design of housing and provide better social facilities.

✱ Help inadequate parents and problem families.

✱ Instill a rejection and distaste for drug taking.

✱ Train the unemployed in a variety of skills.

✱ Legislate against the indulgers in pornography.

✱ Remove children under threat from cruel parents, violence or abuse.

✱ Inspire and motivate children to get fulfilment from helping others.

✱ Encourage positive role models in the community for young people to look up to.

* Form more housing associations to provide low cost housing for young married couples.

* Find community projects in which to involve young people and from which they can obtain fulfilment.

* Provide more social clubs and functions for young people to meet in pleasant surroundings.

* Persuade local businesses to provide job experience for those leaving school.

* Tackle racial issues by regular meetings between those of different races and faiths.

* Provide facilities for the care of the old and the frail, also places where they can meet and socialise.

* Sporting facilities should be available in close proximity to all housing estates.

* Tackle the drug pushers by joint community and police action

* Support for teachers to instill respect and caring attitudes in their pupils.

* Actively encourage industry to settle in deprived areas.

* Social Services to target disadvantaged families so community care facilities can be applied.

* Special constabulary to patrol streets and estates to befriend young people and tackle hooliganism and crime at source.

* Joint partnerships between parents, teachers and school governors to encourage positive aspirations in children.

✴ Extensive publicity to obtain community volunteers by forming a question, 'what are you doing for your community?'

POLITICAL SCENARIO AND BEYOND

Politicians of every shade are far too remote from the electorate they represent, and should they have entered politics as a vocation with ideas to improve the quality of life, the party political machine soon crushes any positive creativity.

The antics of politicians on our TV screens clearly shows ineptitude for addressing serious social problems. There is a belief, too, that the daily inter-party bickering and negative dialogue is instrumental in creating aggressive stances in our relationships with each other.

It is no wonder that the British public is looking for a positive revaluation of how democracy should work in Britain. One of these is in the embryo stage right now.

There is now a growing belief that dynamic solving of social deprivation can only come from local communities and regional government. In effect, a new breed of democratic government is on the cards and it will take the form of Community Management, which will bring dynamism and pride into communities as never before.

In effect, the dominating role of central government will be reversed with the regions being responsible for their own prosperity and social harmony. Already there are movements towards these goals, these being described in the next chapter.

Part Seven

DYNAMIC COMMUNITY MANAGEMENT

Now is the time to plan positive ways of managing our country's affairs using holistic considerations, both in the planning and in the execution of them. The target is the eradication of subcultures in Britain and creating a more just society, something which must cross all shades of party politics.

The success of this social challenge could well be a pilot scheme for the whole world.

In 1995, an all party meeting in Birmingham enthusiastically applauded the idea of devolving much of the power from government at Westminster and handing it to the regions and communities. In effect, there would be a partnership between the government, the individual and the community. This would mean drastic decentralising of government as we know it, and a handing over of many responsibilities to the regions.

In effect, "self management" communities would be formed with all agencies adopting a caring responsibility towards those in their midst who are vulnerable to being deprived of life's qualities.

Just as householders who are house owners show special pride in their home, so people and agencies would become self-motivated to work together for their community and solve problems in a spirit of camaraderie.

People of all ages would become enthusiastic to become involved in fulfilling projects such as building low cost housing for the homeless, caring for the aged, and creating leisure activities for young people.

Initiatives for business and job creation would be fostered with innovation and creativity.

Several pilot schemes incorporating these suggestions are already under way. They are described in more detail within the next chapter

URBAN VILLAGE SCHEMES

Whilst better parenting and positive outlets for bored youngsters go a long way to solving the problems in deprived communities, there are environmental factors which affect the quality of life.

Stark unfriendly buildings, devoid of character and without gardens, trees and social amenities all contribute to the depressive living conditions some unfortunate people have to endure.

Urban Village Schemes are being planned to alleviate many of these problems in conjunction with other positive measures. One such scheme is outlined in an Urban Village Charter which is the basis for others to emulate. It provides the means for people to live in a harmonious environment where both young and old people can communicate, meet their own kind and be proud of their own community.

It is supported by numerous public figures together with environmentalists, business people, sociologists, town planners and charitable organisations. Government from Whitehall is seen more as a partner than an overseer.

Pilot schemes already show that dynamic pride and enthusiasm can develop if communities are given the power over their own destiny.

The Urban Village Charter gives a list of positive proposals:-

* People at present living as tenants in council tenement flats will be offered ownership, in new cheerful accommodation.
* Each tenement block will form a residents' association, and elect a spokesperson to represent members at local community meetings.
* Grim courtyards will be replaced by pleasant green areas, suitably landscaped.
* Roads will be planted with trees and the general effect will be broad tree-lined avenues. At fifty metre intervals, road "calmers" will be introduced to prevent speeding. Cycling paths will encourage healthier means of travelling for children and adults alike.
* Schools, shopping precincts, places of entertainment and job opportunities will all be generated locally, enabling most facilities to be reached on foot or bicycle.

* There will be better amenities for caring for the old, the fragile, and mentally ill, also facilities for nursing mothers and playschool areas where mothers can leave their children in safety.

* Companies with financial incentives will be encouraged to set up business, within easy travelling distance of "Urban Villages." In this way, time-wasting commuting will be reduced to a minimum, less fossil fuel used and pollutive exhaust fumes reduced.

* A plentiful range of sporting and outdoor activities, close or within a few miles of the town area, will be provided by a number of dedicated sporting enthusiasts. Young children and teenagers will be constantly approached to participate in challenging sports in order to wean them away from the negative types of excitement, which are all too prevalent.

* There will be a new close co-operation between schools, parents, police and social services. Experience has shown that young people who are likely to go astray, can be helped early and long before they have become candidates for borstal.

Naturally, large sums of money will be required to implement the above. But Urban Village Communities generate their own wealth by better 'house keeping', avoiding expensive bureaucracy, and making savings in a relatively crime-free society.

Successful Urban Village schemes will be a blue print for others to adopt.

MEDIA RESPONSIBILITIES

A large amount of the substance which gushes from the media is tarnished with violence, arrogance, sex, cynicism and innuendo. In our hearts we know it is not right, but we accept it all with a shrug and a comment, "that's how it is these days".

It could be described as a creeping tentacle which squeezes out the spiritual regard one human being has for another. But the effect on young minds which absorb exciting and lurid material is cumulative and inherited so that information presented "quietly, sensibly and without exaggeration" is seen as boring by the next generation.

Aspirations expressed in words, such as ethics, unselfishness, justice, kindness, politeness are seen to be rather old fashioned and therefore it becomes fashionable, even macho, to rebel against them.

Only the older generation can sense that we are losing our sensitivity in a violent society. An example of "grey callousness" is portrayed in a television programme, entitled, "You've Been Framed", when comical mishaps are recorded on amateur videos. A number of incidents which brought roars of laughter from a studio audience, must have caused intense pain to the persons involved. Both the programme director and the viewers appeared to lack sensitivity. Those burying the dead in a concentration camp were heard to comment, "at first seeing so much death was terrible but after a while, bodies became things".

What can we do then to reverse this trend?

People should start demanding a "balanced media" with more news and features depicting positive events to balance the negative ones. Some regional newspapers and radio stations are already doing that very thing!

Here is a challenge to the newspaper world:-

"Calling all those with media influence and who are unhappy with the direction negative style media is taking us. Publish a new national newspaper entitled, "Positive Daily News". It should be stimulating but in a positive manner, truthful, fair, creative and balanced. Progressive news and innovative ideas for a better world would be its hall mark".

There is a ground swell of people just waiting for that publication to appear!

LEISURE ACTIVITIES... UNLIMITED

All people, young and old alike, need self respect and a feeling of positive achievement in some form or other. If they are bored and frustrated, self respect can take a curious twist. A voice inside says, "right, I shall get respect and will demand it from others. I shall be noticed regardless!". In an inner city environment, young people succeed in being noticed and we are reminded of this by vandalism, graffiti, petty theft, joy riding, and hooliganism. It is the food of the budding criminal.

A more "depressing" voice will say "what's the use, my life is not worth living!". Those who succumb to this "message" are likely candidates for drug addiction, depression and mental illness.

In the chapter "Targets for social healing", one solution to the problems stands out above the others, and that is the vital need to constantly involve young adolescents in positive activities to such an extent that there is little room for the negatives ones to enter the equation.

From playschool onwards, children should "stumble" on positive pastimes, remembering we are in competition with computer games and violent scenes on TV and video screens, which are also exciting. Leisure pursuits must therefore be both stimulating and challenging.

But even unselfish pursuits, if not exactly exciting, can be enjoyable. At an early age, one can see the joy of caring in the antics of toddlers playing "doctors and nurses". The soul development process begins with "teddy bear hugs" and ends with "compassion for the needy".

The following list of leisure activities for young people should therefore be "dangled under noses" from dawn to dusk.

Sporting activities. Football, Swimming, Basketball, Mountain biking, Hang gliding, Ballooning, Windsurfing, Pot holing, Stock car racing, Ice hockey, Skating, Horse riding, Volley ball, Cricket, Pony trekking, Sponsored runs, Rock climbing, Go karting, Athletics, Gymnastics.

Helping in the community. Sponsored walks for charity, Doing errands for old people, Planting trees and flowers, Collecting litter and material for recycling, Supporting one's favourite charity.

Music/Dancing/Singing/Acting. Learning to play a musical instrument, Joining a pop group, Ballroom dancing, Joining an amateur dramatic society, Making one's own video.

Electronics/Computers/Crafts/Woodcraft. Young people can become involved in all these subjects from council sponsored schemes and private ones run by the voluntary sector. Colleges and local industry can also provide facilities for young people to study many of these subjects and/or obtain work experience in them.

Nature. Joining wildlife trust activities, Following nature trails, Rambling, Renovating canals, Forest management, Gardening, Planting trees, Visiting farms, Monitoring pollution.

Children from inner cities should be able to leave the concrete jungle and "lose themselves" in the natural environment of woodlands and the countryside

Social clubs. There is a need for more clubs where young people can meet and socialise in a positive atmosphere, where activities such as table tennis, darts, snooker, bowls, chess and dancing are available. Such clubs should be organised by enthusiastic volunteers from the local community and be places where the whole family are made to feel welcome and secure.

Outings for children. All young children from deprived families, including the handicapped, orphans, and those with special needs should have regular outings to supplement play-school. They could be taken to theme parks, community woodlands, adventure playgrounds, swimming pools or the seaside.

HELP LINES FOR MOTHERS

Vast numbers of young women are quite unprepared to meet the responsibilities of motherhood, and the following support and advice is essential for their own and their children's well-being.

Basic nutritional education should be available, preferably even before conception! The diet of many living in poor communities is unbalanced and a recipe for ill health.

Expectant mothers need to know exactly what is a balanced diet and what can be bought to fulfil this on a low budget. This should be a subject for all teenagers in their last year at school, and they should be tested to prove their understanding of it.

Behaviour patterns and hyperactivity in young children have been traced to excessive junk food. Recently, some young, uncontrollable children, expelled from school, became perfectly 'normal' following some basic vitamins and zinc being introduced into their diets. The connection between hooliganism and diet has yet to be proved, but since animals become aggressive when malnourished, there is a probable correlation

Bringing up children is difficult even with a healthy diet and a bank balance, but the problems escalate when you cannot make ends meet and you are living in semi-squalor with violence on your doorstep.

It is obvious that to bring up law abiding and polite children in a hostile and aggressive environment, is virtually impossible without some assistance.

The trip wires for good parenting in our modern society are all too many to be ignored and it seems sensible that a parental guidance course should be compulsory for everybody with no stigma attached to it. Furthermore, it should be viewed as a valued part of extended education.

For those living in deprived city areas, there should be accessible family help centres. Mothers should never feel guilty or lose self-esteem by attending them. If you or I had the task of bringing up a family in the stark conditions of an inner city, we would welcome a helping hand.

Being provided

Being deprived

SOCIAL SERVICES

In addition to their usual roles, Social Services can become family counsellors and are in a valuable position to see where help and support is needed most. They can spot tell tale patterns of problems in the family by children's behaviour even when they are still in their nappies. Neglected or abused toddlers do not thrive, are hyperactive, accident prone and resistant to toilet training.

It might seem to be an invasion of privacy, but to reverse the underclass, every family must be monitored in the interests of the children. They are the future!

Social Services are grossly under-funded and short of trained welfare staff. Their role is invaluable and they should be paid accordingly.

COMMUNITY FORESTS

The enthusiasm for wildlife continues to have a knock-on effect. This is reflected in a number of "community forests" being planted, twelve at this moment of time. It is planned that wildlife and woodlands should be on the doorstep of millions of city dwellers.

Sensing that greening of urban areas would be well received, the Countryside and Forestry Commission have planned for a number of these forests, largely using derelict industrial land close to major towns and cities. This will involve the planting of many thousands of deciduous broad leafed trees so as to produce a mosaic of woodlands, lakes, paths and hedgerows.

Their plan is to provide numerous wildlife havens, but also important for city dwellers, recreational areas and attractive landscapes. These to provide job opportunities and healthy leisure pursuits.

Nature, expressed in woodlands, plants and wildlife, has a healing quality and makes the quality of life more meaningful.

ROLES OF THE POLICE

The main function of the police is seen to be maintaining law and order and catching criminals, but they have a definite role to play in reversing the subculture trend. They see what is happening at first hand as they patrol the streets. But so often young people see the police as the "enemy", who align themselves with the "haves" of this world. Unfortunately, they do at times, give that very impression in their attitude to juveniles when seen in groups on the streets. Police therefore must take on the role of "father figures" and not just law enforcers.

Special constables, perhaps part time, voluntary and trained to give a positive image of "support" rather than "arrest", should be seen on the streets. They should be befriending parents and children alike. Such special constables would provide a vital link between social services, schools and parents, all parties regularly meeting to discuss strategy.

Social involvement of the police is imperative, for they are the ideal medium to "hold the pulse" of behaviour trends and receive respect from those who seek law and order.

ROLES OF THE "EDUCATORS"

Education has become a battleground between the "traditionalists", who are obsessed with the 3 R's, and others who see character building as the main object in education.

Naturally, we cannot just have good-natured people unless they have the ability to "put two and two together", but the idea that one cannot have an holistic education without the 3 R's suffering, is defeatist and erroneous.

It is essential that all children, without exception, have access to play school from 3 years old, where "education for living" commences. The basis for a fair society starts even when children are still in nappies, but they must be inspired to think of orderliness as a normal growing up procedure and not a punishment. In effect, respect, tidiness and politeness need to be praised so they raise the self-worth level.

The school syllabus can include holistic themes of kindness, love and justice. Such "messages" can be introduced within religious, history and geography lessons, without degrading learning quality. But school assembly provides an ideal stage for expressing holistic thoughts, and putting progressive ideas into children's minds.

Older children can be challenged to discuss and write about such matters as "what is important for a better world?" An essay on this would exercise one of the 3Rs, but with a bonus of holistic expression, something which remains in the mind for applying it in a practical fashion in later life.

Schools/Teachers/Parents... a Bond

So often we hear of disputes and conflicts between teachers, parents and government. This is so very negative. We are "playing around" with the future generation and if you think it through, the well-being of the country as a whole is at stake if we allow this to continue.

It has already been shown how teachers and school governors can involve parents in their children's education with a "partnership" style of friendly co-operation. Parents even come into the classes sometimes and sit alongside their children or even help the teachers in various ways.

But before children reach puberty, they should receive instruction in parenthood. We teach children sex and how babies come but not how "good parents are born"

The confusion between the factions hides the fact that all parties are really "on the same side", with the end products of education being to produce knowledgeable, but thoughtful, well balanced and caring human beings.

ROLES OF RELIGIONS

Religious agencies can and do already play a part in bringing positive values into deprived communities, but it would be more effective if there was enthusiasm for finding avenues to prevent polarisation of the faiths.

Most religions express care and love for fellow human beings but service to others is not a uniquely Christian ethic. Taking this one stage further, a multicultural camaraderie must be the ultimate target in every community, so the plight of any one racial sector is felt to concern the whole.

One cannot enforce a caring attitude, but one can encourage the growth of goodwill by meeting people from different cultural backgrounds and viewing their problems from their point of view.

Local leaders of the faiths can do wonders for their people if they can "shout from the roof tops" all that is common amongst the mix of cultures rather than emphasise the differences.

Summing up. Religious agencies in deprived communities, providing they encourage interfaith camaraderie, can play a vital role when working alongside teachers, social workers, police and the caring agencies to give positive meaning to people who have lost their way in life,

SUPPORT FROM INDUSTRY AND COMMERCE

All businesses receive a bewildering assortment of charity mailings and to check which donations should take priority over others is a problem, but to reverse the underclass trend, industry can play a vital role. Local businesses can work closely alongside community employment centres and provide training and encouragement. But pressure should be also exerted on national management to give more generous incentives for industry to move into areas of high unemployment and deprivation.

Every appropriate firm can take on a quota of young trainees and give them work experience.

There should be incentives in every town for setting up new local industries, and encouragement given to young people to start up enterprises of their own. Established firms and high street banks can help to show them how to set about doing this.

Never underestimate the ability of young people who are disadvantaged. It is not charity they want, for that can be soul-destroying, but a helping hand with some training and know-how from those with experience.

The situation requires a message to business people. It is this, "Please come forward with positive ideas and join others in the most important social healing process of the century."

SUPPORT FROM THE GENERAL PUBLIC

Once the ideas for reversing the underclass trend in Britain has been seen to be feasible, enthusiasm will grow and progressive minded people will appear on the scene like magic.

The nature of the underclass challenge will have special appeal to the general public. It is likely to be women who will first take the initiative, as they have more sensitivity about their children's welfare and are the first to see how "life on the streets" affects their children

There will be immense support from those charities already involved in caring and social welfare. Religious institutions will give maximum backing.

As they have in the past, public figures in sport and entertainment would sponsor activities to raise funds.

There will be lobbying in parliament to provide financial support for the regions, and applications will be made for EEC funding.

Once the general public have got "the message" and the feel for wanting to participate in some way, enthusiasm will snow-ball. This will be reflected in all areas of media publicity.

The world will be watching with anticipation.

Britain is not the leading power it used to be, and there is a malaise of low self-esteem, but this project, which addresses social injustice on a huge scale, has the means of giving its people an immense uplift in pride and achievement.

But there is also a bonus for the planet. A British achievement will encourage other governments to give self respect to their young people who have also fallen by the wayside in the scramble for materialism.

In the meantime, the world will be watching us with anticipation.

The care of "young humanity" is an international obligation and if we have found the "know how" of making capitalism fairer and holistically acceptable, it belongs to the world.

What are the basic messages for all those intent on improving the quality of life for the many thousands of families caught up in the sub-culture of our inner cities?

First find your dynamic organiser to bring together the various agencies listed above, and inspire them to work in unison.

Never be dismayed by set-backs. Always think... is there another way? If you have faith, ideas will arrive thick and fast in most extraordinary ways.

Your enthusiasm and confidence will win over any sceptics, and your positive outlook will catch on in a wave of support.

The potential for projects with positive spiritual values is unlimited!

Part Seven

ADMINISTRATION PLAN
and Division of Responsibilities

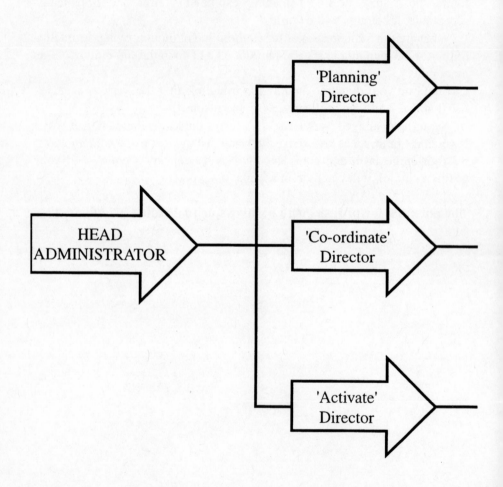

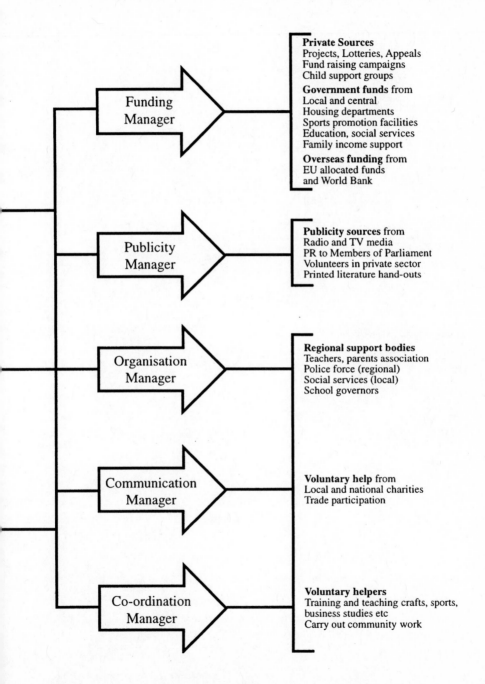

Funding Manager

Private Sources
Projects, Lotteries, Appeals
Fund raising campaigns
Child support groups
Government funds from
Local and central
Housing departments
Sports promotion facilities
Education, social services
Family income support
Overseas funding from
EU allocated funds
and World Bank

Publicity Manager

Publicity sources from
Radio and TV media
PR to Members of Parliament
Volunteers in private sector
Printed literature hand-outs

Organisation Manager

Regional support bodies
Teachers, parents association
Police force (regional)
Social services (local)
School governors

Communication Manager

Voluntary help from
Local and national charities
Trade participation

Co-ordination Manager

Voluntary helpers
Training and teaching crafts, sports,
business studies etc
Carry out community work

ECOLOGY AND THE SPIRITUAL CONNECTION

THE FEMININE FACTOR

LET US SEARCH through our history books for women who have enslaved weak nations, murdered helpless people and invented weapons of mass destruction. With men seemingly to be more bestial than women, one might well come to a conclusion. If God is love, and to be sure it is true, then God is more likely to be feminine than masculine.

Whoever is 'in command' of our destiny in the coming millennium, it is safe to prophesise that women will be taking a leading role in the evolution of the human spirit.

Surprisingly, it is the science of Ecology which brings this to light, because the inter-relationship of all living creatures includes caring and respect. This implies that justice and compassion should be extended to the more vulnerable creatures on the planet, and women show a marked sensitivity in this area.

There is a strong movement under the name of Ecofeminism, whose members are all concerned with the environment. They are most determined not to be swayed by commercial interests, and are dominant in lobbying their members of parliament, particularly on green issues and when cruelty to animals is involved.

Compassion in World Farming, largely organised by women, carries considerable weight in European circles on animal rights issues. It is highly respected, and has been responsible for improving animal welfare, and helping to eliminate cruel factory farming practices.

But there is a another aspect to ecology which involves the discordant relationships between different races and tribes of the human species. If the custodians of the earth are themselves in disarray, the future of the world could be in jeopardy, therefore peaceful trends between countries and religious factions need every possible support.

Women feel a strong revulsion to the cruelties of war, more so than men who initiate the conflicts in the first place.

When an expectant mother feels a stirring within her body, she is aware of the divinity and beauty of the process. There is spiritual value to the new life and it becomes instinctive to feel very protective towards it throughout childhood and beyond. People portray this caring element by their activities in 'Save the children', 'Help line', 'Children in need', 'Adopt a child ' and similar charities.

Should a mother lose her child in an accident, she 'feels' for other mothers who could experience the same devastation and actively takes steps to try and prevent such accidents happening again.

Women's hearts 'bleed' more readily when they are faced with scenes of starving children trying in vain to obtain milk from their mothers' breasts because they feel the desolation of the mother and the hungry infant.

The largest group of nurses and health workers in crisis areas of Africa are women from Ireland. During the potato famine at the turn of the century, millions died of starvation. The suffering and anguish of mothers seeing their children die from hunger had entered the souls of the following generation.

Women are more peace-loving and sensitive to the horrors of war for similar reasons. Recently, a number of peace initiatives inspired by women were formed. One in particular, called 'Through the heart to peace', was especially active during the Bosnian crisis. They braved gunfire in Sarajevo to provide relief for the stressed inhabitants. All such groups were shocked at the needless killing and maiming of innocent people, and felt the urge to do something positive to alleviate the suffering.

History books confirm repeatedly that men initiate conflicts and so often it is women and children who suffer the anguish resulting from them.

In Northern Ireland it is women from both Christian denominations who lead peace marches. One might wonder why their religious leaders cannot bury their differences, and help the peace process more effectively.

It would appear that men often hesitate to negotiate with peaceful gestures as this is a sign of weakness in the macho warrior image which they bestow on themselves. Fraternity, along with the term 'do-gooders' sounds weak. Harshness and dominance sound strong!

Women in particular have always been the most vocal in the CND movement. They suffered rough treatment when nuclear brinkmanship was the order of the day during the 'cold war'.

At a recent large 'Peace on Earth' gathering at Wembley (UK), when approximately 6000 people from numerous countries pledged their thoughts and prayers for world harmony, at least 80% of those attending were women.

Women on the whole are more sympathetic to positively helping young people who have gone astray. They are able to say ' that could be my child'. Like the Quakers, they are quicker and more eager to look for the good in people.

It is noticeable that the 'lock them up brigade' and the passionate supporters of capital punishment are almost all of the male gender.

Even when young people have taken to murder, the norm is for all people to feel revengeful rather than forgiving, but an extraordinary exception was recorded recently. When a school master, Philip Lawrence, was killed by a teenager, the male establishment demanded a life sentence, but his wife pleaded for better facilities and education for young people in deprived areas. Her thoughts were directed to reducing the violent culture and not retribution for the crime.

Summing up. The science of Ecology deals with the relationship between all living creatures, their modes of life and the effect they have on their surroundings. It is a 'holistic science' because the spiritual connection is clear to see.

We are all part of nature and responsible for its well being and if we are not at peace with ourselves, we cannot be good custodians in a wider context.

Part Eight

The Positive Spirit philosophy looks ahead when all humans, men and women alike, learn to live in harmony, and view discord as very old fashioned.

At this moment in time, such a scenario may appear unlikely, but behind the scenes there are signs of a new era with compassion and justice being the norm for civilised humans.

Gentler natures regularly cross the divide of the sexes and may they continue to do so.

'KINDER FOOD'

THE CYNICS LIKE to class those who care about their diet, as food fads. But one should be remind that it was a fad of the Victorian age which devitalised our stable diet, bread, by taking all the roughage and many of the vitamins from it. White bread and sugar appeared to be 'purer and cleaner', a fad indeed!

Kinder food is an expression which could apply to those who have not yet become vegetarians but feel animals should be reared humanely until their execution.

It applies to calves reared in tiny crates, kept in the dark, and fed with a special diet to give their flesh a pale tint. This being most favoured by the customers across the water. How much more humane would it be for the calves to remain with their mothers for at least a few weeks, but one can be ashamed to belong to the human race when one learns that they are separated when only one day old. They cry for their mothers, and spend most of their time in their crates, licking and nuzzling each other for company. It is to the credit of the RSPCA and Compassion in World Farming that new European legislation bans the live export of these pathetic creatures from British ports.

Human concentration camps have already been described as barbaric, but factory farms are only now being discussed in the same terms. It is most certainly an overdue sentiment. In factory farming, barbarism and greed go side by side, because it is cheap meat which drives all parties to this abomination. In fairness, if the consumer could see at first hand the cruelties, they would willingly pay that small amount more for 'cruel free' meat, eggs etc., and, as one person put it, shoppers would think more with their 'souls' and less with their 'purses'.

But these cruelties continue to this very day because farmers, over many years, have become callous due to commercial pressures, and shoppers in the supermarket live in ignorance about what really goes on behind closed doors on the factory farms. It is gratifying therefore to know that these cruelties will be outlawed within a decade or so, because already a new Freedom Food labelling has just been introduced by the RSPCA. The ideals on which the Freedom Food is based, are as follows:-

Farm animals should have,

Freedom from fear and distress.
Freedom from pain, injury and disease.
Freedom from hunger and thirst.
Freedom from discomfort.
Freedom to express normal behaviour.

The RSPCA will be monitoring and assessing the sources of meat bought by the food trades and the packages will be labelled Freedom Food if they meet the necessary criteria.

But 'kinder' food could also apply to grain and vegetables which if not saturated with pesticides and herbicides, would be 'kinder' to the human animal, to wildlife, fish and the natural habitat, all of which suffer in the food chain.

The pollutants of the industrial age are additionally 'unkind ' to the ozone layer with trees and wildlife down below having to cope with the acid rain.

However, many of these ecological blunders may also soon be described in the past tense, because the green movement continues to impose pressure on policy makers to be more mindful of the environment and less of the economic advantages. Biological pest control, filtering of factory smoke, organic and free-range farming, are just a few of the positive trends on the horizon.

It is all part of a new age of wholesome thinking, wholesome from the point of view of realising that the world is a 'living whole' and a 'living sore' in one spot on the planet contributes to an illness of its whole.

But compassion for the 'human animal' has also taken a surprising turn in the last few decades. We are now made more aware of human suffering from all corners of the earth. Without doubt, satellite television has helped to trigger our compassion more effectively than written reports of the tragedies. Yet, we must not be complacent. It is still shameful to see grain and butter mountains in the West when people are starving in other parts of the globe.

With taste buds tuned to flesh consumption, 'kinder' food will involve producing 'vegetable burgers' with different "meat" flavours. I am convinced that a hundred years from now, vegetarianism will be so commonplace that meat eating will be the exception rather than the rule.

Finally, with the coming population explosion, there is an economic reason for reducing meat consumption. We may be forced to adopt vegetarianism by heavily taxing meat for the following reason, seven times as many people can be sustained from eating the food we give to animals than eating the animals themselves!

Summing up the spiritual implications of this chapter:-

Animals are sentient beings and feel pain exactly as we do. Rabbits, mice and guinea pigs cannot reply to questions such as 'will you agree to this experiment because it saves human lives?'

Callous attitudes towards our fellow creatures is totally opposite to the sentiments expressed within the philosophy of Positive Spirit.

Do not forget, we are part of nature, and mistreatment of the animal family is like being cruel to a member of our own family.

MEAT OR VEG

ANCIENT JAWS of primitive man show that sustenance largely came from consuming flesh. But this does not infer that meat was the first choice. Clearly, edible vegetation was not always on hand in sufficient amounts to sustain a hungry family.

The relationship between vegetarianism and human behaviour is not immediately obvious. Some believe that without meat in our diet we would lose our 'get up and go' mentality, something which we proudly believe makes for success and achievement. But this cannot be substantiated because vegetarians also produce Olympic winners, so we are not likely to become 'vegetable wimps" just because we leave meat off the diet.

All animals are defensive against predators and instinctively fight to protect their young. To some extent, we have the same situation when we fight 'just wars', attacking predators to protect the human family.

But it may be argued that the 'balance of nature' requires savagery. For example, insects are kept in check by frogs, bats and birds, which are in turn controlled in numbers by hawks, snakes, etc,. However, this type of savagery is based on survival of their species and killing to live, when your diet is another living creature, is therefore not bestial but unfortunate for the victim, albeit necessary.

A study of flesh-eating humanity down the ages, and possible aggressiveness related to it, would be interesting, but we cannot escape the fact that the majority of animals with a vegetarian diet are less savage than their meat-eating counterparts. To support this view I have listed two groupings in the animal kingdom and separated the quiet, more peaceful ones from the more savage variety:-

Herbivorous Animals	Carnivorous Animals
Cows	Wolves
Squirrels	Snakes
Rabbits	Tigers
Elephants	Jackals
Sheep	Vultures
Antelope	Crocodiles
Horses	Hyenas

Are we what we eat?

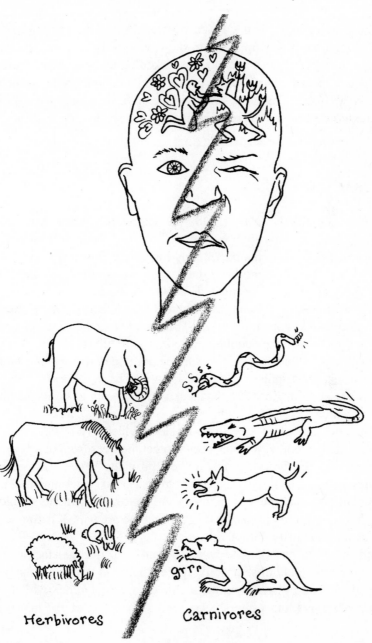

Herbivores   Carnivores

Those living prior to the 1950s will recall how most butchers used to hang animal carcasses up in their shop windows. But this is rarer now because the sight of flesh and blood is sickening to the new generation. The conclusion must be that young people feel uncomfortable about killing animals for food. This is a sensitivity with far-reaching possibilities for humankind because there are no boundaries closed to compassion.

NATURAL SELECTION

FROM DARWIN ONWARDS, the expression 'natural selection' is bandied about regularly to show how all life has developed from the earliest single cells, right up to the present day intricate life-forms.

Whether Darwin's theories stand the test of time, is questionable, particularly as there are spiritual elements to consider.

The wondrous and beautiful creatures which inhabit our planet thrive and multiply in astonishing ways. They work together and rely on each other just as though they communicate in a joint effort.

The wings of one moth are so well camouflaged that when it alights on a tree trunk, it is indistinguishable from the bark. Likewise, one insect swings out at an angle when threatened and appears to be identical to the twig on which it rests.

There are ant colonies in South America which live in trees and form a mutual arrangement with them. They protect the trees from other animals in exchange for the accommodation they provide. This is the science of Ecology when all living creatures are seen to communicate and be dependant on each other for their very existence. Humankind should show some humility in this respect and not forget we are part of nature and only one species amongst a billion others.

But there are questions to which no-one can give satisfactory replies. The expression 'natural selection' typifies the trend to explain nature, as if we worked hand in hand with the architect and the builder, whilst in truth we are observers and often abusers. Here are some of the questions we should be asking ourselves:-

1. How can anyone explain the existence of billions of life-forms in purely scientific terms?

2. What intelligence is at work organising the ecological balance between the life-forms?

3. Is there communication, constructive thought and instincts at work in all living organisms?

We cannot provide satisfactory explanations to the mysteries of creation without including a strong spiritual element. This brings humility onto the scene, something which scientists, who regularly 'play God', should be reminded about it.

One belief is that a vast biological 'computer' with spiritual 'software' is continually creating the design and 'hardware' for the evolutionary process. Life forms 'tune in' to absorb creative thoughts for on-going stages of development.

It might seem inappropriate to use the word computer in the context of God's creations, but it is man who has copied the master creator of life and there is no original computed thought that has not gone on before.

It is believed that vast amounts of 'know how' have been accumulating from the beginning of time, thus enabling life to become increasingly sophisticated, ingenious, beautiful and enjoyable for those who can take advantage of it..

God has given us the spiritual tools to 'naturally select' the means of completing our evolutionary journey, and just as millions of creatures have evolved to near perfection, unlimited Positive Spirit will enable us to do likewise.

Part Eight

THIS EARTH IS PRECIOUS

In 1854, the "Great White Chief" in Washington made an offer for a large area of Indian land and promised a 'reservation' for the Indian people.

Chief Seattle's reply, published here in full, has been described as the most beautiful and profound statement on the environment ever made.

"How can you buy or sell the sky, the warmth of the land? The idea is strange to us.

If we do not own the freshness of the air and the sparkle of the water, how can you buy them?"

All Sacred

Every part of this Earth is sacred to my people.

Every shining pine needle, every sandy shore, every mist in the dark woods, every clearing and humming insect is holy in the memory and experience of my people. The sap which courses through the trees carries the memories of the red man.

The white man's dead forget the country of their birth when they go to walk among the stars. Our dead never forget this beautiful earth, for it is the mother of the red man.

We are part of the earth and it is part of us.

The perfumed flowers are our sisters; the deer, the horse, the great eagle, these are our brothers.

The rocky crests, the juices in the meadows, the body heat of the pony, and man - all belong to the same family.

Not Easy

So, when the Great Chief in Washington sends word that he wishes to buy our land, he asks much of us. The Great Chief sends word he will reserve us a place so that we can live comfortably to ourselves.

He will be our father and we will be his children. So we will consider your offer to buy our land.

But it will not be easy. For this land is sacred to us.

This shining water that moves in the streams and rivers is not just water, but the blood of our ancestors.

If we sell you land, you must remember that it is sacred, and you must teach your children that it is sacred and that each ghostly reflection in the clear water of the lakes tells of events and memories in the life of my people.

The water's murmur is the voice of my father's father.

Kindness

The rivers are our brothers, they quench our thirst. The rivers carry our canoes, and feed our children. If we sell you our land, you must remember, and teach your children, that the rivers are our brothers, and yours, and you must henceforth give the rivers the kindness you would give any brother.

We know that the white man does not understand our ways. One portion of land is the same to him as the next, for he is a stranger who comes in the night and takes from the land whatever he needs.

The Earth is not his brother, but his enemy, and when he has conquered it, he moves on.

He leaves his father's graves behind, and he does not care. He kidnaps the earth from his children, and he does not care.

His father's grave, and his children's birthright, are forgotten. He treats his mother, the earth, and his brother, the sky as things to be bought, plundered, sold like sheep or bright beads.

His appetite will devour the earth and leave behind only a desert.

I do not know. Our ways are different from your ways. The sight of your cities pains the eyes of the red man. But perhaps it is because the red man is a savage and does not understand.

There is no quiet place in the white man's cities. No place to hear the unfurling of leaves in spring, or the rustle of an insect's wings.

But perhaps it is because I am a savage and do not understand.

The clatter only seems to insult the ears. And what is there to life if a man cannot hear the lonely cry of the whip-poorwill or the arguments of the frogs around a pond at night? I am a red man and do not understand.

The Indian prefers the soft sound of the wind darting over the face of a pond, and the smell of the wind itself, cleaned by a midday rain, or scented with the pinion pine.

Precious

The air is precious to the red man, for all things share the same breath - the beast, the tree, the man, they all share the same breath.

The white man does not seem to notice the air he breathes. Like a man dying for many days, he is numb to the stench. But if we sell you our land, you must remember that the air is precious to us, that the air shares its spirit with all the life it supports. The wind that give our grandfather his first breath also receives his last sigh.

And if we sell you our land, you must keep it apart and sacred, as a place where even the white man can go to taste the wind that is sweetened by the meadow's flowers.

One Condition

So we will consider your offer to buy our land. If we decide to accept, I will make one condition. The white man must treat the beasts of this land as his brothers.

I am a savage and I do not understand any other way.

I have seen a thousand rotting buffaloes on the prairie, left by the white man who shot them from a passing train.

I am a savage and I do not understand how the smoking iron horse can be more important than the buffalo that we kill only to stay alive.

What is man without the beasts? If all the beasts were gone, man would die from a great loneliness of spirit.

For whatever happens to the beasts, soon happens to man. All things are connected.

The Ashes

You must teach your children that the ground beneath their feet is the ashes of your grandfathers. So that they will respect the land, tell your children that the earth is rich with the lives of our kin.

Teach your children what we have taught our children, that the earth is our mother.

Whatever befalls the earth, befalls the sons of the earth. If men spit upon the ground, they spit upon themselves.

This we know...The earth does not belong to man; man belongs to the earth...This we know.

All things are connected like the blood which unites one family.
All things are connected.

Whatever befalls the earth befalls the sons of the earth. Man did not weave the web of life: he is merely a strand in it. Whatever he does to the web, he does to himself.

Even the white man, whose God walks and talks with him as friend to friend, cannot be exempt from the common destiny.

We may be brothers after all. We shall see.

One thing we know, which the white man may one day discover - our God is the same God.

You may think now that you own Him as you wish to own our land; but you cannot. He is the God of man, and His compassion is equal for the red man and the white.

This earth is precious to Him, and to harm the earth is to heap contempt on its Creator.

The whites too shall pass; perhaps sooner than all other tribes.
Contaminate your bed, and you will one night suffocate in your own waste.

But in your perishing you will shine brightly, fired by the strength of the God who brought you to this land and for some special purpose gave you dominion over this land and over the red man.

That destiny is a mystery to us, for we do not understand when the buffalo are all slaughtered, the wild horses are tamed, the secret corners of the forest heavy with scent of many men, and the view of the ripe hills blotted by talking wires.

Part Eight

Where is the thicket?...Gone!
Where is the eagle?...Gone!
Where is the end of living and the beginning of survival?

Comments from the author. We owe a lot to Chief Seattle. His protesting
words expose the follies and injustices of an earlier age. He will be glad to
know that the White Man now recognises the errors of his ways and a new
found respect for Mother Earth is growing as never before.

THOSE HEALING FORCES ON CALL

DIY PSYCHOLOGY WORKS

SUGGEST TO SOMEONE that they need psychological treatment when he or she claims to be mentally sound, and you would get a rude response, but the fact remains that we all sway from logic at times and behave quite out of character. We excuse ourselves by blaming problems, pressures and circumstances beyond our control. This can apply to the layman, the academic and even those with the highest IQ in the land.

Intelligence does not open doors to tranquillity. Indeed temporary instability appears in the home, in the work place and in politics. On the road we see it portrayed in so called road rage. We see it in the warring factions in Africa, Europe, the Middle East and India when extraordinary small incidents spark massive reaction. One recent example was the opening of a small stone tunnel in Jerusalem which almost restarted a Middle East war.

But it helps to find solutions to world problems if we face our own behaviour patterns. Let us face it, pressures and problems in our own private world can get the better of us, when our normal temperament, logic and politeness leave us. Usually there is a someone who acts as a peacemaker to bring us back to normality. But if that someone is in the same predicament, a negative trend develops. We see this in some organisations where the whole staff, from the MD down to the tea lady, is rude to each other.

How often have you gone into a shop and sensed a negative atmosphere? It can be the tone of voice or facial expression of the shop assistant.

The nonsense of it all is the misconception that negative effects of modern life are inevitable, and that what we have created we must endure.

Humans are 'their own worst enemy' and yet there are simple solutions to 90% of the problems which are of the self induced variety. For an example, when you meet up with a rude shopkeeper, telephone operator or taxi driver, what are your reactions? Fifteen people out of twenty react in one of the following ways:-

1) Give him a piece of your mind in anger (when you take your anger home with you!)
2) Feel inwardly upset and depressed (when you take your depression home with you!)

The above reactions propagate negative feelings like a virus, and you are likely to take them out on your family, the cat or the next person you meet. If you are sensitive you will just feel miserable. What you need to do is to practice reacting in a sympathetic way to people who are rude, as though they had 'toothaches of the mind' and you were there to soothe the pain. The following scenario may help those intent on becoming a DIY 'mind soother':-

You are trying to park your car in a narrow space when your bumper lightly engages the one behind you. The driver leans out and says 'can't you bloody drive'? Your reply could be: 'Somebody has upset you this morning for you to be so rude. No damage has been done whatsoever. Try to be more pleasant, it costs so little. Take care!'. But many would reply with an obscenity, when both parties would be stressed with anger. One must learn to be a 'peacemaker' which negates a tit for tat reaction to such behaviour.

People are unpleasant, rude, cynical and unkind because they have usually received the same treatment at some stage and they are 'getting their own back'. But to react with sympathy, when one is on the receiving end of such unpleasantness, is difficult, because it has been engraved in one's mind that 'attack is the best means of defence'. It is therefore necessary to adopt a self-challenging nature which says 'I want to heal unhappiness in whatever form it shows itself'

When one disarms negative dialogue, one has become an unqualified psychologist, but, more important, the soul is given a boost, because there was more concern for that rude person than the effect that rudeness had on you!

One has not bottled up resentment at not 'giving as good as you got', because there is pride in the peacemaking role and self esteem has been given a fillip. This is the spiritual aspect of psychology.

Such peacemaking gestures need to cross all borders to heal the many thousands of people who are sick with hate. If each person can portray peace at a personal level, nation can speak peace unto nation and the tit for tat revenge factor can be neutralised.

There are scores of ways of making humans more reasonable and loveable, but it seems sensible to start 'on our own doorstep' and work outwards into the world of disorder.

ARE YOU IN DESPAIR?

DESPAIR CAN MEAN different things to different people.

A starving African is in despair to survive, but, in the West, the word despair often refers to the feelings of a person who has been made redundant, or who cannot hold down a job. He or she feels a lack of self esteem and self- confidence. But the common denominator of worthiness in having a paid job, is a narrow concept. True worthiness is based on how you value yourself as a human being and your ability to be a valuable member of the human race. Being paid for ones labour is helpful but has no bearing on ones value to the world. Five thousand charities at this very moment await your telephone call!

However, there are some amongst us who feel in despair for reasons which have no apparent self-help remedy. I refer to those who are suffering from marital problems, violence, abuse, homelessness, harassment, illness, loneliness, depression, or just lovelessness.

When you are in such despair and you have tried all the usual remedies, you may be uplifted to know that you can call on spiritual help outside traditional sources. Providing your shout for help is sincere and not causing hurt to anyone, you can tap into a 'help line' circuit, somewhat similar to the Samaritans on a BT circuit. One need not be religious for this spiritual connection, but it will help the tuning in process if you have a strong faith in all that's good in the world. Within a few days, possibly earlier, help will arrive in unexpected ways, and it will not be your imagination that you feel 'someone is looking after you'. It will be a fact! Do not expect the help to come immediately, but be patient. It will come in various forms. For instance:-

✳ The illness, which seemed so serious, improves dramatically. Life seems rosier.
✳ A threat which seemed inevitable, disappears overnight.
✳ A grim situation was removed by the kind intervention of a friend.
✳ Unexpectedly a letter arrives which changes desolation into something you can handle.
✳ Your loneliness dissolves because you have been persuaded to join a social club and have found new friends.

To some, the concept of a spiritual thought-healing process is a new experience. Others recognise spiritual healing for they either believe prayer works through their religion or have had 'experiences' to support the reality of Divine Power.

What is clear is that there are millions of unhappy souls who need help, and they should know this is available to them.

Just like the national electricity grid, one can draw on this power, but it also requires thousands of souls to act as 'giving agents'. Givers act like postmen, they can either deliver 'spiritual packets' direct to the needy or to an 'international spiritual grid', from which goodwill, love and compassion are permanently on tap for those who pray for it.

To the 'givers' I therefore plead, 'if you are comparatively comfortable, fit and itching to do something for the world, you are needed!' That little spark of God in your being is valuable and capable of growing in an astonishing way by just being used.

To the 'receivers', I say, 'if you are in true despair, do not doubt that Divine Power will come to your assistance in some form or other. Just pray and have faith. You will be heard and be astonished!'

Note. The transmission of thought in a healing context is described in depth within the next chapter, entitled 'Thought Options'

THOUGHT OPTIONS

WE ALL ACCEPT quite readily that our computer-style brains send electrical messages down our nerves to move our limbs and heal our bruises, but to suggest we can direct our thoughts to send healing forces to benefit others, brings us into the areas of the spirit world where science becomes entangled with religion and the paranormal.

Irrespective of those who class mystical matters as 'hocus pocus', there are now faculties within universities seriously researching these matters.

One belief stands out above others, and that is that there are powers of thought far beyond those involved in verbal communication.

Everything points to thought forces being a form of electrical waves, travelling on frequencies not measurable by conventional means. They have much in common with the network of radio, TV and telephonic systems, but we should not overlook the natural ability of some animals, such as birds, mammals and fish, to communicate beyond accepted viewing and hearing distances. Indeed, we may yet learn from nature that the paranormal is quite normal and we have been looking too long at the 'dissecting table' in the laboratory for explanations.

Any discoveries about thought forces, which can increase the input of holistic wisdom and peace, must be welcomed with open arms. As the various facets under study are so varied, I have listed them in groupings, in spite of their overlapping relationships.

Instinctive thought.

The word 'instinct' is often used to describe how natural senses enter the genes, without any premeditation.

For instance, a newly-born child instinctively reaches for its mother's breast, having used the umbilical cord for sustenance an hour previously. It is said that this is an instinct built into the genes, yet somehow an intelligent decision has been made. But it is impossible to say where instinct stops and reasoning thoughts take over.

Animals, such as the great white geese, and mammals, travel vast distances across the world to breed and feed. Salmon, likewise, perform amazing feats, swimming halfway across the world and finally fighting upstream to spawn! The word, 'instinct', tells us that the creatures seem to know exactly what they are doing and why. This is an instinct integrated with skill to negotiate the varying conditions of current, wind, sea, tides etc. It is far more likely that they are using some form of natural guiding mechanism to perform these feats, one which man could not simulate without modern electronic gadgetry.

Could it be that animals have the sensory perception to read ley lines and plot their path from those electrical force fields which cover the earth's surface like a labyrinth?

Dogs have been shown to become excited when their masters leave to come home, irrespective of flexible working hours. Scientists believe there is a Morphic Field of sensory perception involved, something which may apply to the animal kingdom at large.

A chameleon 'instinctively' changes it's colour to melt into the background and fool the predators. But to dismiss the idea that there is a degree of conscious reasoning behind the instinct, is avoiding the question, namely, 'who is in charge of the operation?'

No-one can dismiss the existence of a master designer and creator and we should be eternally humble about this. Those who get excessively inspired with thoughts of conquering nature, should dwell on the fact that humans are just one of multi-billion life forms on this earth and some humility is needed.

Instinct should be telling us a few home truths, and one is that we are part of nature, and that more 'advanced' creatures are examining our antics, and wondering how a life form called man, can be so proud and yet simultaneously self-destructive!

Human thought forces.

How often do you hear the expression, 'you must be reading my mind'

Thought reading is commonly accepted as being possible but is so easily faked that the feat is usually believed to be a conjuring trick.

There is an induced thought process, called brain washing, which is a form of 'educational hypnotism', in that people can be gradually persuaded to hold views out of character with their normal life stances. This can be menacing because mind control destroys free thought, something that everyone values in the free world. But there are grey areas, such as the re-education of delinquent children, when intense pressure is applied to change their values from negative to positive ones. This raises the question as to where education stops and brain washing start?

Education is thought to be the acquisition of knowledge, but knowledge is not always factual and can be manipulated by the establishment to enforce ideas which are deemed to be truthful but, in fact, are anything but so.

Some people are more vulnerable than others to thought persuasion. For instance, if groups of people are frustrated following an injustice, imagined or otherwise, they are vulnerable to a persuasive orator who can infuse ideas of a negative soul destroying variety. Under such circumstances, small protests can lead to mob violence and on the international scene, relatively small disputes can escalate into warlike situations.

When a whole population is seriously demoralised then 'mass thought infection' can change millions of people into zombies. No better example of this was the growth of Hitler within a Germany demoralised with a worthless currency. A whole country was brainwashed into allowing its leaders to perform hideous cruelties under the delusion of racial superiority. After the war, the inhabitants were genuinely stunned at their own betrayal of human dignity and compassion.

In Britain today, mobs of hooligans can create havoc on the football terraces. Parents say, 'we don't know what came over him, he is not like that normally'.

In North Borneo, researchers found that once a small group of monkeys had learnt how to perform a new function, a whole species in a wide area of the forest suddenly absorbed the technique. Once more, we see a case of Morphic Field transmission which could also apply to the contagious element in human thought and behaviour.

Loving thoughts.

I have described the negative side of human thought forces, but there is a huge untapped source of loving thoughts which the human soul can access.

Loving thoughts, outside the sexual aspect, can in one phrase be described as 'unselfish feelings of wanting to like, and be liked, simultaneously, and being prepared to think and act to perpetuate the feelings'

The 'orgasm' of the soul takes place when the child arrives in the mother's arms, and it prospers or falters from then on. At this point, loving thoughts need nurturing.

The 'soul development process' in the PS philosophy would not be possible without a base of universal goodwill, confirmed by the fact that the vast majority of people are reasonable, and have no wish to be unkind or uncaring unless provoked into being so. But this base is too weak to withstand the problems of world societies, many of which have been created by selfish greed.

The whole purpose of this new philosophy is centred around promoting unselfish service for humankind on a scale which defies present logic. This book tries to become a kick-starting mechanism to establish loving thoughts into human behaviour.

SPIRITUAL HEALING

THE DEFINITION OF HEALING has several meanings. The dictionary quotes 'restoring to health' and 'making sound or wholesome'. Wholesome is the most appropriate word, because being really healthy requires one to be 'wholly' well in body, mind and spirit.

Whatever healing method is applied, it is a question of giving nature a helping hand to 'prime the battery'. This expression is more meaningful than generally realised because our bodies are full of minute cells, electrically charged. If we are weak from ill health, old age or malnourished, our 'batteries need recharging'. This attitude to healing is not readily accepted in the Western world because of its unscientific leanings and healing practices here, largely rely on drugs and surgery, with a notable absence of preventative medicine.

It is quite extraordinary that no in-depth study appears to have been made about the "substance of health" rather than the "presence of disease". For instance; why are wild animals and certain tribes in the world so resistant to the diseases which we accept as inevitable? The secret of immunity seems to centre round nutrition and life style.

The preoccupation with curing disease rather than preventing it, is surely one of the most absurd and expensive trends of modern medicine.

Age-old beliefs are now coming to the surface that natural remedies, both herbals and spiritual, can heal more effectively than most of the conventional ones used in the Western hemisphere.

But other remedies of a more controversial nature are being recognised. Increasingly, cures are being found for a variety of ailments, which work in unexplained ways. They include acupuncture, homeopathy, and aromatherapy, their success being reflected in their acceptance as effective treatment by the NHS for a variety of complaints.

In the early 20th century, healing by unconventional means, now described as alternative medicine, were inclined to be ridiculed and suspect, practitioners being labelled, carte blanche, as 'quacks' and 'charlatans'. Not so now. People in high places and on occasions, doctors themselves, use alternative remedies as a first choice rather than second, but usually in a rather clandestine fashion.

Part Nine

Recently, hypnotherapists stunned the medical profession when several terminal cancer patients were restored to normal health.

It seems inevitable that spiritual healing, which includes psychic healing, will soon join the list of alternative remedies freely available as more people than ever before are turning to spiritual healing when all else has failed. But it is a complex subject and only the basics are described in this chapter.

Faith healing.

This can be divided into three categories:-

* Self-healing by faith.

* Distant healing.

* Healing by "touch".

Self-healing. Disregarding those people who attend to their own minor disorders, there are cases of people with serious illnesses who have 'willed themselves' to be cured without consulting anybody. Cancerous growths in advanced stages have been known to wither away to the astonishment of doctors.

In such instances outside healing forces, electrical in nature, are thought to have entered and reinforced the body's own healing and immune system. Determination and confidence of a cure, appear to gather the forces from without in some unexplained way.

Those who aspire to a religious faith may find it easier to pull in such healing forces, but evidence shows that many people who have faith in a divine power (irrespective of their style of God worship) can pray to be healed and will be able to tap into a 'healing force field'.

Distant healing. This is often described as 'absent healing' and refers to healing energy conveyed from a distance.

It can come from a person or a group of people, praying or *willing* for a recovery in that person. It helps the recipient to have faith in the successful outcome of the 'treatment', but it is by no means essential. Such healing forces can be transmitted through space to its destination. In one sense it can be compared to the communication link-up via space satellite.

There is strong evidence that peaceful solutions to wars and conflicts are resolved by spiritual forces healing the 'demented souls' of leaders seeking revenge and power.

The former terrorist cum-prime minister of South Africa, Nelson Mandela, brings this idea into focus. Not only had he healed the rift between blacks and whites in his own country but he inspired all races in his world tour. His sincerity in expressing healing love and fraternity to a listening world sowed an aura of peace into millions of souls. The cumulative effect of 'prophets' like Mandela pave the way for that universal Positive Spirit we are to welcome in the coming millennium.

One might enquire as to the sender of these peace-loving forces. One little recognised source is the international network of light workers, whose sole aim is to saturate the world with aspirations of love, compassion, justice and composure. Peace makers, who suddenly turn up, arrive on the scene and defuse apparent irreconcilable conflicts, may well have been directed by the healing forces of light workers, who are themselves directed by their Positive Spirit.

Even people just 'thinking peace' inject a small element of healing to violent situations, but earnestly praying for it, whether it be from Church, Synagogue, Mosque or from one's sitting room, can help to heal the disruptive activities of mankind most effectively. But no one status of person has a monopoly in being able to raise healing energy.

At all times it must be stressed the 'healer' is acting as a 'distributor' of divine forces, and should not claim any shade of divinity. Be cautious if healers demand high fees. Charlatans proliferate!

Most Clerics, Rabbis, and Mullahs believe such healing can only be done through their own brand of faith, but evidence shows that if sincere and unselfish aims are involved, the powers of healing are universal and open to all those with compassion and goodwill. If someone likes to call this witchcraft, or mumbo jumbo, so be it!

Healing by 'touch'. Healing power often comes through the finger tips, when electrical forces emanate from the healer's body and enter the patient through the hands. One usually feels a tingling sensation or heat at point of contact. Most healers now do not physically touch the subject, but feel the aura or bio-force which surrounds the person, and 'see' the area needing treatment. Such healing powers are recorded from the bible up to this present day and, in due course, it will receive the respectability it deserves.

Once more, the nature of a true healer is that he or she must be a sincere compassionate person without egoistic motives.

Whilst the healing process is helped by the subject having faith in the treatment, it is by no means essential. Sick animals have been treated successfully with spiritual 'hands-on' healing.

Many people could have the power to heal if they had the faith and audacity to go along that route. This is supported by Kirlian photographic equipment which can portray the auric electric field surrounding our bodies. People with proven 'healing powers' are recognised by the style of light emanating from their hands, this being clearly seen on photographic plates, but the genuine "hands-on" healers of today, who can "see and feel" the medical problems of their patients, need no photography to prove their worth. Claims of cures constantly arrive and baffle the official medical world.

Christians mostly believe in the 'hands-on miracles' described in the New Testament. It should not degrade their value in knowing that scientific explanations for such healing may arrive in due course.

Food for thought. Without doubt, it will be confirmed officially that spiritually inspired forces are on tap to heal our minds and bodies, and thus confirm that humans of every shade and race are in reality 'Children of God', when no special groups should dominate others.

The human spirit is in a transitional state and every avenue of healing is welcome in the Coming New Age of Truth.

Let us pray for the faiths of the world to come together as soon as possible and acknowledge a God of Peace & Love, on call to heal the world.

PART TEN

SCIENCE FICTION, FACT OR FUTURE?

FORCES THAT MATTER

THE AUTHOR WAS TAUGHT at school that stone and steel were lifeless objects, but now we learn that there is life of an electrical kind in everything we touch, pick up and view. In effect, the whole world is one complex 'force-field of energy'.

Even objects such as diamonds, plastics, and the common house brick, are really, 'living matter', not in the image of a life form as we know it, but containing electrical particles which cluster together in thousands of variations.

You and I have every reason to be confused because every scientific discovery exposes more mysteries.

For instance, we now hear that minute organisms, a thousand times smaller than a pin head, have a degree of intelligence, a mind-boggling thought indeed!

But some humility is overdue as we try to emulate nature. The microchip with its vast store of information is a point in question. Are not our brains packed full of 'natural microchips' and should we not be working on ourselves to make our 'chips more user friendly', as the expression goes?

The world and the universe is packed full of forces. Understanding them is one thing, using them wisely is another. Electricity in itself is still not fully understood, although we use it in a variety of ways. It can be galvanic, static, high cycle, single phase, three phase, low frequency, radionic, thermal, positive, negative, and magnetic. There are electrical waves (heart), electric storms (weather). Should we not include radio waves, x-rays, infra red rays and what about those pictures on our TV screens, and the 'messages' running down our nerves from the brain?

There are natural forces accepted by science, but reluctantly, because explanations have not been formalised. One example is the electrical force which emanates from our hands, this being exploited by dowsers (deviners) who are often employed to pinpoint the movement of water, oil and minerals below ground. The forked rod held between both hands reacts dramatically when an 'electrical' bridge is made between the dowser and the substance below. Some dowsers can 'read' the electrical discharges from energy fields which interlace the earth's surface. These are called ley lines, the value of which have been recognised by the Chinese for thousands of years (dragon lines). An important building is always built where the 'energy force field' is strongest, which is often on a hill top or where lines cross each other. But now there is a belief the body of the earth itself is one huge power house of electrical energy.

Some dowsers use pendulums for health diagnosis with astonishing results. By focusing on a person from a distance with the presence of a 'witness', (i.e. hair sample or blood sample) an experienced dowser is able to receive pendulum responses to a range of questions about that person's health.

Clearly, the world is saturated with electric forces, and even those from outer space need to be considered. For instance, bio-dynamic farmers, which include the most renowned wine growers in France, plan their growing techniques according to moon phases and positions of the planets. Documented evidence has shown that electrical forces from outer space improve leaf growth during the waxing of the moon, but enhance root growth during the waning period. The myth that madness relates in some way to the moon, has some substance. Mental institutions confirm that patients are difficult during the full moon phase.

Life energy forces of the human body have been recognised and used within cultures all over the world. Often, they are used for healing purposes with the Chinese calling it Ch'i. The Yogis call it Prana. In Hawaii, they call it Mana. The ancient Egyptians called it Ka. The Western spiritual sciences call it Aura, Bio-force, and Bio-radionic energy.

These energy forces can be captured on camera in the form of an aura. The high frequency radiation photography used in this process, called Kirlian photographic process, highlights the strong life force of a healthy person and, conversely, the weaker one of an ill one. A person holding a pebble can be seen to transfer energy to it. Likewise a person can transfer his or her energy to another person needing to overcome a disability. The recipient often feels a tingling or heat from the healer in the process. What is most remarkable is that the hands of people with a high degree of healing energy (or bio-radionic energy) show up yellow on a photographic film. Such people are believed to have natural healing powers of which they are totally unaware. The chapter entitled, Spiritual Healing, deals with this subject in more detail.

Summing up the implications of this chapter.

Forces proliferate across the world and universe, whether we fully understand them is not so important. It is how we use them that is the vital issue.

The future of mankind centres round positive resolutions, such as:-

"All existing forces and new found sources of energy must be examined with 'holistic eyes' to see if they can be of positive benefit to all mankind in the pursuit of peace, compassion and mutual understanding."

ROLE OF SCIENTISTS

RESPECT FOR SCIENCE on the whole is not what it should be. This is reflected in the low intake of students taking up careers in science. The reasons for this are not difficult to spot.

The Western world has bolstered its economy by selling modern weapons of destruction to those who might have settled their disputes amicably. This suggests to young people that scientists have 'blood on their hands'.

Factory farming symbolises cruelty to animals and chemists running amok poisoning the food chain.

In a green-conscious society, which reaches right down to the primary school, the scientist appears as the villain responsible for the destruction of the ozone layer and polluting the sea.

Some blame the Victorian age which brought us the benefits of fossil fuels and assumed that the by-products of the industries could be flushed away into vast areas of air and water, something that God had provided for such a purpose.

It all sounds as though the scientists are the wicked ones and the world could well be rid of them. This is where one can fall into the trap of fragmented thinking, because blame is so often misplaced when only symptoms are focused upon.

Scientists of industry design and produce what demand dictates, and the root cause of many problems we heap on ourselves, point to education. Those who insist that the 3 Rs are the magic solution to a better world, should dwell on the fact that the most brutal dictators in Africa had a 'good' British education.

Politicians are expected to guide scientists in positive directions, but they are motivated to placate people within their constituency rather than display a wise ethical role. For example, if an inventor designed a super effective land-mine and it provided jobs in an area of high unemployment, the export potential would be given a higher priority than the consideration that the mines would be destroying innocent lives for years to come. If our education system could build ethics into the school curricula, the very idea of a super-destructive land mine would not have been born, let alone

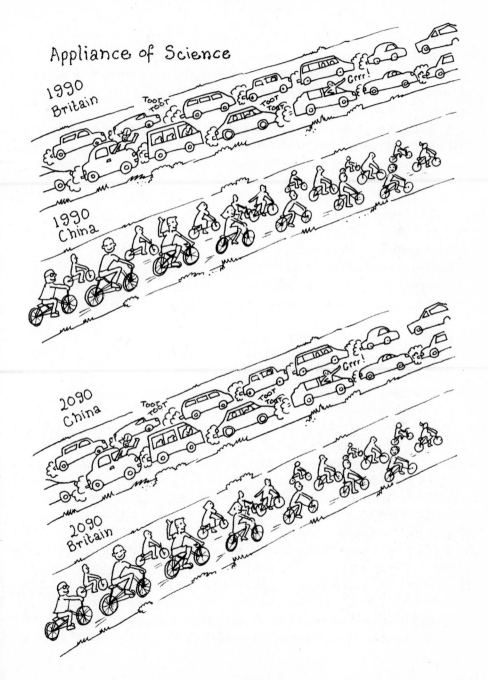

considered as a means of reducing dole queues.

Clearly then, it is up to the people, which includes you and I, to pressurise governments and our educationists, to introduce holistic awareness into the 3 Rs, so when our young people leave school to enter the world of science, ethical considerations get more priority.

Pressure groups have been extraordinarily successful in influencing sluggish governments to act on progressive issues.

But reforms take time to come to fruition, and in the meantime, scientific research and development should be minutely scrutinised to ensure their output will truly benefit mankind.

A list of positive suggestions pinned to their bed-ends, could include -

✳ Invent products which do not pollute.
✳ Design more products which are recyclable.
✳ Develop sources of power which are sustainable
✳ Invent a cheap method of converting sea water into fresh water
   so deserts can flourish.
✳ Build electric cars or ones which run on water or hydrogen.
✳ Replace harmful pesticides and herbicides with biological ones
   which do no harm to the food chain.
✳ Develop an efficient fast public transport system using magnetic
   monorail technology.

We know that scientists are human and possess that common urge to discover and achieve, but clearly they need their energies channelled into healthy and ethical directions.

Even the scientists who designed atom bombs, such as Ritblott and Zacharov of Russia, eventually campaigned for their banning after they saw the terrible consequences of their products.

As the 21st century approaches, the philosophy of Positive Spirit will be needing to bring both scientists and politicians into an instinctive moral frame of mind. This can be encouraged if each of them say before retiring:-

"Please God, do not allow my ambitions and commercial pressures to affect my responsibilities for the safekeeping of the world and the precious life dwelling on it."

But the philosophy of Positive Spirit aims to create an instinctive sense of responsibility in souls, so that we have no need to say this prayer. We will awaken with those holistic sentiments built into our thinking process.

Soul-ess Science?

PART ELEVEN

PREDICTIONS FOR THE 21ST CENTURY

BEAMING PEACE... 2010 AD

WITHIN THE LIFETIME of your children there will be radio and television channels beaming holistic values across the world. This will be a 'United Nations' project for the new millennium, the purpose of which is to create an enthusiasm for 'people to talk peace unto people' and not merely for heads of nations to do so.

But the concept of talking peace will spread in a wider sense, as most countries will be setting up their own stations to beam peaceful initiatives to their own people.

The advances in hi-tech communication will allow anyone in the world with a cheap Televisor to talk face to face to each other. No longer will the expense of Television or Internet be denying the poor the chance of seeing how the other three-quarters of the world live. Naturally, negative activities on the world scene will be graphically displayed but this will trigger positive thoughts, such as 'we must avoid going along this route'.

With Televisors costing less than a pair of shoes, those suffering injustices will find the means of opening their heart to a billion 'all seeing all listening public'. Like never before, communities who have created harmony by solving social problems will, at a stroke, be able to tell the world how they did it, and thus spread a copycat process of holistic living.

We are ten years into the third millennium and we can see the philosophy of Positive Spirit steadily gaining ground on a universal basis. Here is one regional station, based in central England, beaming positive ideas to a million listener/viewers on 280 telecycles.

Simon Scott. "This is Simon Scott from Tele-radio PS, Bristol, England, on 280 telecycles.

We send a welcome to all Tele-radio viewers in the UK and those viewing in from abroad, but first here is a short holistic thought for today.

Let us wake up to the fact that the world is but one country and its citizens are its guardians. Let your problems be our problems!

We have exciting news for you today. The International PS Consortium is agreeing to provide five million Ecu to support our volunteers involved in irrigation schemes in former desert regions of North Africa.

Good news from Holland and Australia too, where we hear PS is catching on fast.

We offer PS enthusiasts across the planet any useful advice we have acquired bearing in mind our lengthier experience of PS progress in the UK, but we warn enthusiasts everywhere about the danger of infiltration by organisations, cults or sects, who see PS as a vehicle to launch their own ideas which may be incompatible with the PS philosophy.

For the benefit of those unfamiliar with the philosophy behind the PS movement, I will briefly explain the basic concepts:-

The philosophy of Positive Spirit aims to bring all people in the world into a common loving fellowship. This means that we are all responsible for each other's welfare, and the suffering of a person ten thousand miles away should concern us just as personally as if it were happening on our doorstep.

There are still pockets of misery and injustice in the world and we are committed to help eradicate these sores of humanity by introducing holistic education and physically helping those in distress. We promote the idea of 'Youth Voluntary Service' when young people become involved in unselfishly helping others less fortunate.

Positive Spirit is not a religion, but is a spiritual emanation which injects our souls with compassion, love, and a desire for justice and tranquillity amongst all humans everywhere.

We are concerned with uniting all those who differ in faith, colour, race and origin, so that the 'world brotherhood of man' is no longer a fantasy. It is something we can look forward to if we all have faith in our cause and are prepared to do something about it.

Naturally, we still have pockets of deprivations in our own country, and I wish to address your attention to some of these from our listeners"

"Hallo once more! This is Simon Scott of Tele-radio PS on 280 Telecycles. Please phone in with your comments or problems now. We await your calls. We have George Willis from Leicester on the line. Good morning George!"

George Willis. "Good morning Simon. I am a Christian, and believe in the sentiments of the PS philosophy 100%, but it seems that they are already built into the Christian faith, so why not just spread Christianity throughout the world?"

Simon Scott. "I hear you George. Your comment comes up quite regularly. Many people confuse the philosophy of PS with Christianity and on the face of it, there are many similarities. The most obvious one is that compassion and love should be built into everything we do.

But one must face it, George, there are some lovely people within every faith, and religions have become divisive because they are fearfully protective. Those who search for the truth about Godliness find themselves happy with the PS philosophy because it seeks total harmony between all humans and every imaginable faith. There should be no discrimination between the souls of this world, and whether one is born in Lapland, India, Kenya or Korea, should not make an iota of difference. We are all members of one human race!

Religious leaders still demand obedience from their followers in their own brand of Godliness. In doing so, believers sometimes feel that they are at liberty to degrade followers of the other faiths. This is one of the remaining setbacks to the 'universal brotherhood of man'.

You see George, man is overwhelmed with independence, adventure, pride, discovery and achievement. He has not fully acquired the means to do these things in harmony with others,

Almost up to this day, faiths have given 'permission' in the hearts of people to do terrible things to others who feel loyal to their own brand of faith. Witness the horrors of 'ethnic cleansing' in 1942 and 1993.

I challenge listeners to cross examine themselves. Have we never found ourselves looking for a scapegoat when things go wrong? It might be the government, or that loud neighbour. Perhaps it is that vulnerable one in the funny clothes who looks 'different'. It might be that one who gets up early to earn his living and seems to make a go of things.

George, your Christian faith is very precious providing you practice what your Saviour preached. You see, we believe that Jesus meant us to revere his ideas and teachings! His martyrdom has created a personality cult which has distorted the 'love thy neighbour' concept, into a permit to 'hate the one who does not show love'. People who feel hated feel unloved and cannot find love in their hearts to express it to others. This is a vicious circle of hating just waiting to be broken by the likes of you and me.

Summing up George, if you can adjust your Christian beliefs to love the non-Christians too, you are already practising the PS philosophy, and being a better Christian in the bargain. No! keep your faith in Christian ideals, they're just great!"

George Willis. "Thank you Simon, I've got the hang of it now, but do you think I can eventually abandon my belief in Christianity if my values are so similar?"

Simon Scott. "Why should you? PS is only an expansion of our religious horizons, so that we can accept others who are 'different' as true brothers, both in words and deeds. The test might be would you risk your life equally in the event of mortal danger to a Christian, Moslem, Jew, Sikh or Buddhist? I'll leave that one with you, George, as I have Janet Sanders from Leeds on the line.

Hallo, Janet, and a good morning to you. Come in please!"

Janet Sanders. "Good morning Simon, I am a primary school teacher, and the philosophy of Positive Spirit appeals to me greatly because I feel I may be able to influence the coming generation if I can sow the seeds of PS in the minds of my youngsters who come from many ethnic backgrounds.

Our children still live in a volatile society round here, and deprivation in our community is still around, although very much improved since 2005, when PS solutions were introduced into the community.

The reason for calling you, is that I need to bring still more of the PS philosophy into my lessons so I can inspire more spirituality within the set curriculum which I am obliged to retain."

Simon Scott. "I see your problem, Janet. There is a booklet now which describes the numerous ways of bringing PS into the forefront of children's minds, both at home and at school, but here are some useful guidelines.

PS can be introduced into the assembly of children at school, and subtly into most lessons. It is quite simple to slip in PS thoughts without deflecting from the curriculum.

For instance, within geography, the concept of each child pretending that he or she was born in another country sows the seed of tolerance for someone who looks different but is really the same 'inside.'

How about a simple essay on 'How I would like to make the world a happier place'? Each child reads out his or her essay and the children are encouraged to discuss their ideas together.

Write in for our free booklet Janet, entitled 'PS and the child', as this covers the areas which will help you.

Next year, you will be pleased to hear, the curriculum is to be changed to include many of the suggestions we recommend for seeding the PS Philosophy into the minds of the very young.

God Bless you and your young pupils!

Must leave you now.

We now come to our prayer session to help those doing great work at the Red Mill Estate in Manchester, England.

I now ask you to clear your minds, retire to a quiet spot and close your eyes. Please pray through your religion, or other agents of God, for strength, wisdom and inspiration to help all who are trying to create harmony on the Red Mill Estate in Manchester. There are hundreds of willing hands who need your PS thought waves, but your help will reach them through the following people who are project leaders.

Your positive thoughts to:-
To John Marsh, who is trying to get support from local builders to construct a community centre.
To Rev. Richard Dale who is organising a boy's club and needs assistants.
To Ibrahim Patel who is organising interfaith discussions to improve community relations.
There will now be a one minute pause, before we take the next caller".......................................

END OF TERM... 2050 AD

THE SCENE IS GREAT BRITAIN in the year 2050. Venue is the National State School in Watford, Hertfordshire. Occasion is the end of term talk by the Headmaster, Mr. Geoffrey Kahn.

In a large assembly hall, dome shaped and solar panelled, approximately 1500 students of both sexes, are seated. They face a central ten foot screen. Mr Kahn appears on a holographic screen sitting relaxed in his living room. His three dimensional image portrays a larger-than-life realism. His voice is conveyed through micro-speakers built into the chairs of the auditorium. Although Mr Kahn is speaking to a large audience, he portrays a sense of speaking to each person individually.

"Today is an exciting time with many of you leaving school and facing challenges of infinite variety.
The main purpose of my message today is to point you in the right direction for a happy, motivated and fulfilling life.
The question about our purpose in life comes up continuously, and I am not going to lecture you on the rights and wrongs of human living. You

know it in your souls without me spelling it out to you.

But be on guard about some of the positive ideals we have taught you here, for they can be undermined by those with selfish aspirations of a past age. You must therefore be spiritually alert to face situations which challenge your soul.

Always recognise your power of introducing Positive Spirit into your decision making, never underestimating the knock-on effect this may have.

Study the latest findings on PS subjects and use them diligently to increase your soul influence in the interests of ethical and spiritual creativeness but always avoid the temptation of imposing PS on those who are not yet ready to receive it. The PS philosophy is not a dogma but an holistic expression of the soul and can be summed up by another sentence, *Positive Spirit comes more readily from the soul pointing outwards than from Spiritual dogma pointing inwards.*

We are all now living in a multi-racial society, but even in these more enlightened times, friction can occur between those of you with varied priorities and ideas of living in accordance with your traditions. Just as a blend of colourful wild flowers prosper side by side in a meadow, so can we humans live side by side with mutual regard for one another. Needless to say, should any of you wish to practice your faith alongside differing ones, it should be accepted amicably and without a hint of malice.

A word of warning from past experience. Built into the human psyches, is an excitive urge to probe, discover and create, typified by our urge to find new worlds in space. Obsessive motivation for achievement and power can squeeze out holistic considerations unless an ethical charter is built into your projects. In this respect, I leave you with the following thoughts to dwell upon:-

Practice trying to build PS philosophy into your thinking process, so it becomes a natural trait in your character. Life will then become more meaningful and enjoyable, and your spirit will enter the souls of others and multiply.

PS spreads by example, with a knock-on effect spreading through the family, the workplace, and the world at large.

Positive Spirit must be seen for what it is, a natural loving energy which comes from the soul into the arena of humanity, with infinite capacity for growth.

Some of you will be finding paid employment, others will become fulfilled by helping those less fortunate than yourselves in such organisations as the World Voluntary Service, or World Harmony Through Service.

Let us spend five minutes in silence to contemplate harmony and loving thoughts."

Mr Kahn disappears from view and is replaced by virtual reality scenes of utmost beauty from around the world, accompanied by a background of inspiring music.

When five minutes have elapsed, the voice of Mr Kahn comes through.

"Please all hold each other's hands to let your bio-forces project with maximum sincerity the following thoughts,

May your Positive Spiritual feelings of love, compassion, and caring prosper, multiply and spread to all corners of this world, so we can live in harmony with each other and all other creatures on our precious planet."

GLOBAL NEIGHBOURS... 2095 AD

IT IS NEW YEARS DAY 2095, and celebrations are happening on an international level as never before. This can be attributed in many ways to technology, which in the past has been viewed as the villain rather than the saviour.

It all centres round hi-tech communication which has brought people together in a remarkable way. Just as the Facsimile and Internet inventions of the last century revolutionised international communication, so the modern hand held Televisor has transforming peoples' outlook on their fellow citizens. This time, the product is there for the masses to use, because the solar powered unit is affordable to 80% of the adult world population.

This latest model permits the user to both speak and see any other person

Global Neighbour 2095 AD

at the press of a button, and there are no running costs involved whatsoever.

But there are political and social aspects of the technology which have had far reaching effects in the development of the poorer countries. Anyone can now tune into other country's news bulletins which are instantly translated into the chosen language for the benefit of the Televisor holder. Deprived and exploited minorities can now become aware of international law relative to their rights. Those at the receiving end of harassment, persecution or cruelty can expose the perpetrators in a flash.

Governments can no longer hide from their responsibilities and there is little escape from those intent on being devious, for the modern Televisor permits those in the remotest parts of the world to express their problems to a listening and seeing world.

It is apparent, too, that there is a feeling of 'togetherness' between countries in spite of diversity of cultures.

Caring and compassion seem not to be restricted to boundaries and this is reflected in a camaraderie between nations, some of whom were barely on speaking terms a century ago. War is now considered to be positively barbaric!

The United Nations, which formerly was anything but united, now lives up to its name in a way never thought possible a few decades ago.

In essence, all developed nations now show genuine concern that people in remote parts of the world are in good shape. The concern is in the form of a reciprocal care factor.

Summing up the implications of 'global neighbour', there is a holistic concept that the human race is beginning to bond together and feel like one family which has been split up through reasons of geography, climate and living conditions.

The human species thrives on achievement and excitement, but whereas, in centuries past, such motivations led to tyranny, greed and crime, consideration for others is now a basic human trait. Holistic resolutions are now gradually being built into our instinctive thought processes. Increasingly, souls automatically 'prod' conscious minds with the ancient holistic saying 'treat others how you would like to be treated', something which was preached but little practised prior to the Age of Enlightenment.

CARING IN ACTION... 2100 AD

WITH THE RAPID advance in visual communication, it will not be long before disasters in foreign lands will be portrayed at lightning speed to billions of people. The 3D images of suffering will surely touch people's souls as never before, and their compassion will generate positive desires to help. With the future-acknowledged power of mass 'thought healing projection', the following report describes the application of this wonderful process.

It is the 21st century. The scenario is in Bangledesh where severe flooding has caused an immense tragedy. Such a tragedy has been prophesied following the global warming and melting of the ice caps, but not on this scale.

The report comes from a leading newspaper of the times.

ALTHOUGH SOME FLOODING REGULARLY OCCURS IN BANGLEDESH, THE WORLD WAS SHOCKED BY THE LACK OF WARNING WHEN HUGE SEAS ENGULFED LARGE AREAS OF THE COUNTRY.

Part Eleven

"As news reached the world, people turned on their Televisors to witness for themselves the horror of people being swept away in swirling waters with little help of rescue.

Aid for the victims was expressed by unparalleled generosity from all corners of the world. The now universal access to Televisors enables people to see graphically what is happening from one end of the planet to the other.

In the UK alone, half a million people donated funds by tele/credit within hours of the event.

Reports are coming in that teachers in schools across the world are interrupting their lessons so prayers of support for the victims can be beamed to the bereaved. They say many of the younger children, who had just been issued with Televisors as an educational aid, were traumatised by the horrific scenes.

The Red Cross Rapid Deployment Force, RCRDF, have already flown in 30 jumbo wing-jets which air-dropped several thousand self-contained living quarters complete with one month's rations for a family of four.

Volunteers who arrived on the scene and befriended survivors, many of them in shock, requested that mass spiritual healing should be directed at set times to alleviate the pain and misery of the injured and those who had lost their loved ones.

Such is the impact on souls of this major disaster that industrial concerns, world-wide, report staff are using their holiday leave to help the survivors.

Furthermore all Light Working and caring agencies have promised practical aid and spiritual support for the injured and bereaved.

National management teams had already made plans to enlarge the operations of the World Disaster Action Force and following this disaster, which surprised scientists who assumed their early warning system was fool-proof, it is certain now that the huge project will now be implemented without delay.

Since the banning of arms at the turn of the century, many armament factories have been searching for alternative products to manufacture. Space station construction has only partly absorbed the large number of unemployed people who were made redundant at that time. However, many thousands of people will now be needed to construct and be employed to run the proposed ten new WAD stations. Earlier, small stations had been used to despatch military forces to world trouble spots. These latest outposts are to be sited at specific points around the world, along with a number of observation posts out in space.

The purpose of the exercise is to be able to react instantly to every possible emergency on the world scene. Within minutes of reports of a disaster, mobile hospitals and homes will be rocketed with pinpoint accuracy to any given spot on the planet, also space jets with vertical landing facilities will rush volunteers to the disaster areas.

We wish to give you the following information for enquiring about friends or relatives caught up in this disaster:-

First give your identity number, then state fullest details after entering the prefix WDA-ENQ. on your Televisors.

For offers of help, enter your identity information and be ready in advance to describe what realistic help you can provide.

We have a special message for you from the Director of the Spiritual Healing Centre at the United Nations, Mrs Ilse Ramali:-

Since the effectiveness and need for prayer has now been accepted by the world at large for the prosperity of the human spirit, I plead that all readers should try to set aside five minutes to send their healing thoughts to the thousands of people who are injured and in severe trauma.

Cascades of healing prayer will greatly help those suffering from their ordeal and the families who have lost their loved ones. Healing times will be announced daily for the following day... blessings to you all."

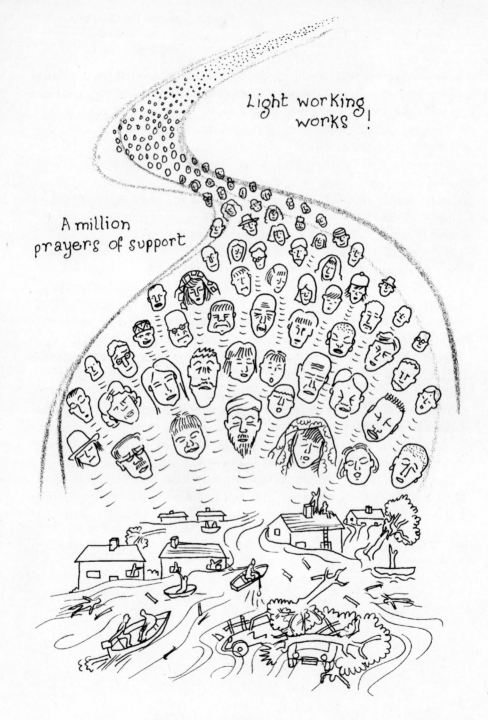

PART TWELVE

POSITIVE SPIRIT NETWORK

The purpose of this book is to encourage the adoption of the Positive Spirit philosophy on a world-wide basis, but during the five year period up to 1997 when this book was first published, it was clear that people of like-minds would like to meet each other, form their own groups and become active participants. My friend, John Crowe, took the initiative and together we founded the Positive Spirit Network.

THE AIMS OF THE NETWORK.
The Positive Spirit Network is a non-profit making concern which has basically four roles to play.

It firstly aims to show how humankind can project and expand that elusive peace and harmony the world needs.

Secondly, it networks all like-minded souls with a view to establishing a positive transformation in human relationships.

Also, it fosters a self developing feeling of concern for others, irrespective of race, religion, colour or status, and a desire to direct charitable thoughts into practical deeds.

Importantly, the Network aims to enhance spiritual evolution through the souls of children with positive aspirations. One of these is that the reason for being in this world is to help others less fortunate and that each and everyone of us has a role to play in the process.

Further information can be obtained from:-

Positive Spirit Network
PO Box 1297, HALSTEAD, Essex CO9 2LW England

PART THIRTEEN

INDEX & INFORMATION SOURCES

Address changes and additions

Updates

Page 2
GOLDEN EAGLE PUBLISHING,
PO Box 10. Llandrindod Wells
Powys, Wales, LDI 5WJ
Email: goldeneaglebooks@talk21.com

Page 277
Fringe Dwellers, PO Box 10
Llandrindod Wells, Powys, LD1 5WJ UK

Glocal 3000 International Communities'
Network PO Box 1015, Corsham, Wilts,
SN13 9FF UK

Page 279
Positive News,5 Picton Enterprise
Centre, Shropshire, SY7 8NF

Removals

Page 278
Kenya Aids Intervention address

Additions

Glocal 3000, Box 1015, Corsham,.................B,E,F,G & I
Wilts, SN13 9FF UK

Heal the Planet-Heal Yourself Network,........B,E,F,G,& I
PO Box 1015,Corsham,Wilts, SN13 9FF, UK.

J.C. Crowe Communications, PO Box10,..........B,E,F,G,& I.
Landrindod Wells,Powys, LDI SWJ, UK

Positive Community Spirit Trust,PO Box 10
Landrindod Wells, Powys, LDI 5WJ. UK..........B,E,F G & I

The New Word Network,..................................B,E,F,G,& I
P O Box 1015, Corsham, Wilts, SWI3 9FF

ADDRESSES

SUBJECT MATTER   **GROUP REFS**

AGENDA 21, RESCUE MISSION PLANET EARTH
See Peace Child International for address _ _ _ _ _ _ _ _ _ _ _ _ _ B,C

BAHAI FAITH
27 Rutland Gate, London, SW71P. Tel: 01438 355983 _ _ _ _ _ _ _ _ G

BATTLEBRIDGE CENTRE
2-6 Battlebridge Road, London, NWl 2TL. Tel:0171 278 7172 _ _ A,C,F

BRAHMA KUMARIS WORLD SPIRITUAL UNIVERSITY
UK Branch, c/o Inner Space, 89 Regent Street, W1.
Tel: 0171 439 3940 _ I

BRITISH SCHOOL OF YOGA
l Hamilton Place, Boston Road, Sleaford, Lincs, NG34 7ES.
Tel: 01529 306851_ I

CENTRE FOR ALTERNATIVE TECHNOLOGY (UK)
Machnlleth, Powys, Wales, SY209AZ _ _ _ _ _ _ _ _ _ _ _ _ _ _ _ C,D

CENTRE FOR INTERNATIONAL PEACE BUILDING
9 West Street, Chipping Norton, Oxon, OX7 5LH.
Tel: 01608 642335. Fax: 0608 44732 _ _ _ _ _ _ _ _ _ _ _ _ _ _ _ B,F

CHANGING THE WORLD
National Youth Agency, 17 Albion Street,Leicester, LE1 6GD
Tel: 0116 285 6789. Fax: 0116 247 1043_ _ _ _ _ _ _ _ _ _ _ _ _ _ _ A

COMPASSION IN WORLD FARMING
Charles House, 5a Charles Street, Petersfield, Hants, GU3 23E
Tel: 01730 264208/269863_ C,D

CREATION SPIRITUALITY
St James Church,197 Picadilly, WIV OLL. Tel: 0171 287 2741 _ _ _ _ I

DEVELOPMENT EDUCATION ASSOCIATION,
3rd Floor, 29 Cowper Street, London EC2A 4AP.
Tel: 0171 490 8108 _ A

ECO NETWORK (UK BRANCH)
8 Beaufort Court, Eagle Close, Ilchester, Somerset, BA22 8JZ.
Tel: 01935 840086 _ C

FINDHORN FOUNDATION
The Park, Findhorn, IV36 OTZ, Scotland.
Tel: (44) 01309 691933. Fax 691833 _ _ _ _ _ _ _ _ _ _ _ _ _ _ _ _ _ I

FIRST PEACE
PO Box 123, Stourbridge, West Midlands, DY12 0WL.
Tel/Fax: 01926 497663 _ A-I, J,L

FOCOLARE
69 Parkway, Welyn Garden City, Herts. Tel/Fax:01707 339 792 _ _ _ _ B

FOOD COMMISSION UK LTD
Freepost KE7564, London, EC23 2DF _ _ _ _ _ _ _ _ _ _ _ _ _ _ _ _ _ D

FORESIGHT (Association for Promotion of Pre-Conception Care)
Old Vicarage, Church Lane,Witley, Surrey, GU85PN _ _ _ _ _ _ _ _ _ A

FOUNTAIN INTERNATIONAL
PO Box 915, Seaford, East Sussex, BN25 ITN _ _ _ _ _ _ _ _ _ _ _ _ I

FRIENDS OF THE EARTH
26 Underwood Street, London, NI 7QJ. Tel: 0171 490 1555 _ _ _ _ C.D

FRINGE DWELLERS
PO Box 3296, Sudbury, Suffolk, CO1O OPL.
Tel/Fax 01787 374001_ A,C,F, G,I

GLOBAL INITIATIVE
CH 3232, Ins. Switzerland. Tel/Fax: (41) 32 313 2458 _ _ _ _ _ _ B,C,D

GOLDEN EAGLE ENTERPRISES
Technologies of Light, PO Box 3296, Sudbury, Suffolk, CO10 0PL.
Tel/Fax: 01787 374001 _ A,F,G,I,J

GREEN NETWORK CHARITABLE TRUST
9 Clairmont Road, Lexden, Colchester, Essex, CO3 5BE.
Tel: 01206 46902/76605 _ C,D

HELSINKI CITIZENS ASSEMBLY
11 Goodwin Street, London, N4 3HQ.
Tel: 0171 272 9092. Fax 0171 272 3044_ _ _ _ _ _ _ _ _ _ _ _ _ B,C,F

HUMAN SCALE EDUCATION
96 Carlingcott, Nr Bath, BA28 A12. Tel/Fax: 01761 433733 _ _ _ A,B,F

INTERFAITH ORGANISATION
5-7 Tavistock Place, London, WCI H9SS. _ _ _ _ _ _ _ _ _ _ _ _ _ G

INTERLINK TRUST (Meditation in schools)
30 Hanover Steps, St George's Fields, London, W2 2YG.
Tel: 0171 7063094 _ A,I

INTERNATIONAL COMMUNITIES NETWORK
P.O.Box 3296, Sudbury, Suffolk, CO1O OPL.
Tel: 01787 374001 _ A,F,G,I

INTERNATIONAL PEACE CENTRE
House of Hope, Shefa-amer, 20200, Israel. _ _ _ _ _ _ _ _ _ _ _ _ B,G

INTERNATIONAL LIGHT FOUNDATION
PO Box 136, Norwich, Norfolk, NR3 3LJ. Tel: 01603 440944 _ _ _ _ _ I

KENYA AIDS INTERVENTION/PREVENTION PROJECT
PO Box 1297, Halstead, Essex. CO9 2LW. Tel: 01787 374001 _ _ C,E,F

KINDRED SPIRIT
Foxhole, Darlington, Totnes, Devon, TQ9 6EB.
Tel: 01803 866686. Fax: 01803 866591 _ _ _ _ _ _ _ _ _ _ _ _ _ _ J,L

LIGHTNET
PO Box 9640, Wanstead, London, E.1.
Tel/Fax: 0181 518 8633 _ I,H,L

LINK-UP
7 The Retreat, Broadway, Worcs, WR12 7DZ. Tel: 01386 852167 _ _ _ L

LOCAL AGENDA 21
c/o LGMB, Arndale House Centre, Luton, LU12TS.
Tel: 01582 451166_ A,B,C,F,J.

LUCIS TRUST
Suite 54, 3 Whitehall Court, London, SW1A 2EF.
Tel: 0171 839 4512. Fax: 0171 839 5575 _ _ _ _ _ _ _ _ _ _ _ _ _ _ I

MPH GROUP (Meditation for Peace, Harmony and Creative Living)
Box 3380, Savyon 56540, Israel. _ _ _ _ _ _ _ _ _ _ _ _ _ _ _ _ _ _ _ I

MULTIFAITH & MULTICULTURAL MEDIATION
4 Woolas Hall, Bredon Hill, Pershore, Worcs, WR10 3DN.
Tel/Fax: 01386 750965_ B,G

NATIONAL FEDERATION OF SPIRITUAL HEALERS
Old Manor Farm Studio, Church Street, Sunbury-on-Thames,
Middx, TW16 6RG. Tel: 01932 783164 _ _ _ _ _ _ _ _ _ _ _ _ _ E,I

NATIONAL FOOD ALLIANCE
5 Worship Street, London, EC2 2BH.
Tel: 0171 628 2442. Fax 0171 628 9329 _ _ _ _ _ _ _ _ _ _ _ _ _ C,D

NATIONAL PEACE COUNCIL
88 Islington High Street, London, N18EG. Tel: 0171 354 5200_ _ _ B,C

NEW ECONOMICS FOUNDATION
1st Floor, Vine Court, 112 Whitechapel Road, London, E1 1JE.
Tel: 0171 377 5696 _F

NEW LIGHT FOUNDATION
Lahaina, 24 Beresford Road, North, E46 EE. Tel: 0181 529 8097 _ _ E,I.

NEWPIN (parent help for neglected children)
35, Sutherland Square, London, SE17 3EE.
Tel: 0171 703 5271. Fax: 0171 701 2560 _ _ _ _ _ _ _ _ _ _ _ _ _ A,D

NIDRA & SANKALPA INSTITUTE
See Satyananda _ I

PARENTS ANOMYNOUS (serious problems)
Tel: 0171 263 8918_ A

PARENT NETWORK (general)
Tel: 0171 485 8535 _ A,D

PEACE CHILD INTERNATIONAL (UK Branch)
The White House, Buntingford, Herts, SG9 9AH.
Tel: 0176 327 4459. Fax: 327 4460 _ _ _ _ _ _ _ _ _ _ _ _ _ B,C,D,F,J

POSITIVE NEWS (Planetary Connections)
Six Bells, Church Street, Bishop's Castle, Shropshire, SY9 5AA.
Tel/Fax.01588 630121/22 _ A-I,J

POSITIVE LIVING GROUP
40 Studland Road, Hanwell, London W7 3QX_ _ _ _ _ _ _ _ _ _ A,B,E,I

PRAYERS FOR PEACE
70 Weymouth Road, Frome, Somerset, BA11 IHJ. Tel: 0373 71317 _ _ I

PRISON PHOENIX TRUST
PO Box 328, Oxford, OXI IPJ. Tel: 01865 798647_ _ _ _ _ _ _ _ _ _ K

PRISON REFORM TRUST
The Old Trading House, 15, Northburgh Street, London, EC1V OAH.
Tel: 0171 251 5070. Fax: 0171 251 5076_ _ _ _ _ _ _ _ _ _ _ _ _ _ K

QUAKER INTERNATIONAL CENTRE
1 Byng Place, London, WC1. Tel: 0171 387 5648 _ _ _ _ _ _ _ _ _ _ G

RELIGIOUS EXPERIENCE RESEARCH
c/o Alister Hardy Trust, Westminster College, Oxford, OX2 9AT.
Tel: 01865 243006, Fax: 441865 and/or 251847 _ _ _ _ _ _ _ _ _ _ E,H,I

RESURGENCE, FORD HOUSE
Hartland, Bideford, Devon, EX39 6EE.
Tel: 01237 441293. Fax: 01237 441203 _ _ _ _ _ _ _ _ _ _ _ _ _ A,I,L.

SATYANDANDA YOGA CENTRE
70 Thurleigh Road, Balham, London SW12. Tel: 0181 673 486 _ _ _ _ I

SCIENCE OF SPIRITUALITY
45 Queen of Denmark Court, Finland Street, London, SE16 ITB
Tel: 0171 231 6705 _ E,G,I

SCIENTIFIC AND MEDICAL NETWORK
Gibliston Mill, Collinsburgh, Leven, Fife, KY9 1JS.
Tel: 0133 340492 Fax: 0133 340491 _ _ _ _ _ _ _ _ _ _ _ _ _ _ _ E,H

SCIENTISTS FOR GLOBAL RESPONSIBILITY
The Business Village, Broomhill Road, London, SW18.
Tel: 0181 871 5175 _ C,F

SOIL ASSOCATION
86 Colston street, Bristol, Avon, BSI 5BB. Tel: 01272 290661 _ _ _ C,D

THEOSOPHICAL SOCIETY (UK)
50 Gloucester Place, London, WH 3HJ. Tel: 0171 935 5265/9261 _ _ G,I

TREE OF LIFE
14 Croftdown Road, Harborne, Birmingham, B17 8RB.
Tel: 0121 427 8250. Fax: 0121 428 4550 _ _ _ _ _ _ _ _ _ _ _ _ _ E,I

TRIANGLES
Suite 54, 3 Whitehall Court, London, SWIA 2E _ _ _ _ _ _ _ _ _ _ _ G,I

UNESCO
Place de Fontenoy, 75732 Paris, 07SP, France. Tel 00331 45681000 _ _ B

UNIVERSAL ALLIANCE
5 Newton, Fowey, Cornwall, PL23 IJY. Tel: 01726 832196 _ _ _ _ _ B,F

UNIVERSAL WORLD HARMONY THROUGH SERVICE
36 Exmouth Road, Stoke, Plymouth, Devon, PLI 40H.
Tel 01752 564987 _ A,B,E,I

VOLUNTEER CENTRE (UK)
PO Box 7, London, W3 6XJ _ K

VIPASSANA MEDITATION, Vipassana Trust, Dhamma, DIPA
Harewood End, Harewood, Herefordshire,HR2 8NG.
Tel: 0189 730234. Fax: 730450 _ _ _ _ _ _ _ _ _ _ _ _ _ _ _ _ _ _ G,I

G L O S S A R Y

ABSENT HEALING

Term given to those who can give spiritual healing without the patient being present and often without their knowledge

ASTRAL PLANE

This is the emotional band of the Earth's electro-magnetic fields. It is the plane where our spirit is believed to go when our physical body dies. Time on this plane is considered non-existent and one can meet passed friends and loved ones in the time of one's memory of them.

AURA

This is the electro-magnetic field surrounding all physical things, which give them life-force. When healing is involved, the description, Bio-force or Radionic Energy is used.

CHAKRAS

These are the energy vortices in the body's electro-magnetic field, traditionally seven in number, which feed the energy into the glands. Chakras of the planet refer to the energy meeting points in the Earth's surface and crust.

DOWSERS

These are people who interact their own electrical emanations with force fields and materials which conduct them, such as water, oil and certain metals. Some diagnostic dowsers can use their energy to diagnose causes of ill health.

DRAGON LINES.

One Chinese expression for Leylines, the importance of which has been recognised in China for thousands of years.

ETHERIC

This is the aspect of the electro-magnetic force field which immediately surrounds our physical body and relates to our health and well-being.

GEOMANCERS

People who have the ability of adjusting the energy flow of Leylines beyond that of dowsers. The practice is common in some far Eastern countries but not so in the Western hemisphere.

GODHEAD

With the numerous religious orders which have their own interpretation of God, there are those who believe that the introduction of a belief in a universal unifying symbol, not replacing, but overseeing the 'other Gods', will be a key in bringing a camaraderie between the different factions of worship.

INTERFAITH

When people or organisations are working to bring those of different religious faiths into harmony and mutual respect of each other.

KARMA

This basically means the "law of learning our lessons". The "lessons" tend to keep repeating themselves, again and again, life after life, until we finally learn them.

LEYLINES

Energy lines, electro-magnetic in nature, which criss-cross the earth's surface and can be tracked by some dowsers. In pre-Christian times, great importance was attached to these when siting buildings (usually at the peak of hills where the energy is strongest).

MEDITATION

A systematic way of relaxing, breathing and controlling the mind, thus allowing higher spiritual dimensions of the self to be accessed.

ORGANIC

By law, the description of organically grown food requires it to have been grown for a minimum of five years without the application of pesticides, herbicides or artificial fertilisers. It also applies now to animals raised on such land but requires the exclusion of any artificial growth substances or medical treatment in the rearing process. Farms are regularly inspected to ensure validity.

PARANORMAL

The term which applies to mystical or unexplained phenomena. Scientists refer to the ease of faking the paranormal for gain. There is, nevertheless, a nucleus of phenomena which are unexplained by a scientific yardstick. However, research suggests that energies connecting mind, body and spirit are not paranormal, but normal. For instance, forms of successful spiritual healing, although still defying conventional medical practices, are becoming recognised. In times to come, belief in the normality of the subject is likely to cross the sciences.

SOUL

This is the spiritual essence of humanity, in both a personal and collective sense. When developed, it has infinite power to bring peace, love and harmony onto the world scene.

This book was due for printing in September but when Princess Diana tragically passed away, the publishers agreed for some last minute changes.

I think readers will agree, Princess Di was, and is, the very essence of what Positive Spirit is all about! Likewise, Mother Teresa, another messenger of love, reminds us that there is an imperfect world waiting for us to do our bit to put it right, each in our own little way! H.S.

.—.